SMART APARTMENTS

SMART APARTMENTS

KÖNEMANN

is an imprint of Frechmann Kolón GmbH
www.frechmann.com

logos

Edito e distribuito in Italia da:
2014 © Logos edizioni
Strada Curtatona 5/2
41126 Modena, Italy
T: +39 059 412 648
commerciale@logos.info
libri.it
logosedizioni.it

Editorial project:
LOFT Publications
Barcelona, Spain
T: +34 93 268 80 88
F: +34 93 268 70 73
loft@loftpublications.com
www.loftpublications.com

© 2014 for this edition: Frechmann Kolón GmbH

Art director: Mireia Casanovas Soley
Editorial coordination: Simone Schleifer
Editor and Texts: Mariana R. Eguaras Etchetto
Layout: Ignasi Gracia Blanco
Translations: Equipo de Edición

ISBN 978-3-86407-370-0
ISBN 978-88-576-0689-7 (Logos, Italy)

Printed in Spain

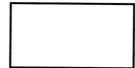

This book looks at a selection of apartments which show a wide variety of architectural and design solutions suitable for different kinds of properties – from a small studio loft to a two or three-storey home. It looks at the work of international designers and architects, taking the reader on a visual journey to see the latest trends in contemporary international design in private homes in big cities all over the world. The book is arranged according to the number of rooms in each apartment, excluding the bathroom and kitchen.

Cet ouvrage rassemble une sélection d'appartements qui présente un vaste éventail de solutions architecturales et décoratives adaptées à différents types de logements : depuis le petit studio d'une pièce à la résidence de deux ou trois étages. Cette sélection reflète le travail d'architectes et de décorateurs des quatre coins du globe et permet au lecteur d'entreprendre un voyage visuel à travers les intérieurs de résidences privées situées dans les grandes villes du monde entier, où l'on retrouve les dernières tendances du design contemporain international. Le livre est organisé en fonction du nombre de pièces en plus de la salle de bains et de la cuisine.

Im vorliegenden Band werden Wohnräume vorgestellt, in denen sich eine breite Vielfalt von – an die jeweiligen wohnlichen Bedingungen angepassten – Design- und Architekturstilen widerspiegelt: angefangen beim Mini-Apartment bis hin zur offen gestalteten, sich über mehrere Etagen erstreckenden Wohnung. Der Leser begibt sich auf eine visuelle Reise durch die von internationalen Designern und Architekten gestalteten Wohnungen in den wichtigsten Städten der Welt, in denen sich die aktuellsten Tendenzen des zeitgenössischen Designs wiederfinden. Das Buch ist nach dem Kriterium der Zimmeranzahl der Wohnung plus Bad und Küche in verschiedene Teile gegliedert.

Dit boek toont appartementen die heel verschillend zijn qua architectuur, ontwerp en grootte. Er zijn eenkamerappartementen in te vinden, maar ook appartementen van twee of drie verdiepingen. In deze selectie is het werk van ontwerpers en architecten uit de hele wereld terug te vinden. De lezer kan een kijkje nemen in de interieurs van privéwoningen in grote wereldsteden om een idee te krijgen van de laatste trends in hedendaags internationaal interieurontwerp. Het boek is ingedeeld aan de hand van het aantal kamers van een appartement, waarbij badkamer en keuken niet worden meegerekend.

Este libro ofrece una selección de apartamentos que presentan una amplia variedad de soluciones en arquitectura y diseño adecuadas a diferentes tipos de viviendas: desde un pequeño apartamento de un solo ambiente a una residencia de dos o tres plantas. El trabajo de diseñadores y arquitectos de todo el mundo queja reflejado en una selección que permite al lector viajar visualmente por los interiores de residencias privadas situadas en importantes ciudades de todo el mundo y donde se exhiben las últimas tendencias del diseño contemporáneo internacional. La división de los capítulos se ha hecho de acuerdo con el número de habitaciones del apartamento, además del cuarto de baño y la cocina.

Questo libro raccoglie una selezione di appartamenti che presentano un'ampia varietà di soluzioni architettoniche e di design per diverse tipologie di abitazioni, dal piccolo monolocale alla grande residenza distribuita su due o tre piani. Questa selezione riflette il lavoro di progettisti e architetti di tutto il mondo e consente al lettore di compiere un viaggio all'interno di alcune residenze private dislocate nelle più importanti città alla scoperta delle ultime tendenze del design contemporaneo internazionale. Il libro è organizzato in base al numero di locali di ciascuna abitazione, bagni e cucine a parte.

Este livro compila uma selecção de apartamentos que apresentam uma ampla variedade de soluções arquitectónicas e de design que se adequam a diferentes tipologias habitacionais: desde pequenos lofts a casas com dois e mais pisos. O trabalho de designers e arquitectos de todo o mundo surge aqui apresentado numa selecção que permite ao leitor viajar visualmente pelo interior de casas privadas de várias cidades do mundo, acompanhando as últimas tendências do design internacional contemporâneo. O livro organiza-se em função do número de divisões de cada apartamento, excluindo-se casas de banho e cozinhas.

Denne bog ser på et udvalg af lejligheder som demonstrerer en bred forskellighed af arkitektoniske og designmæssige løsninger passende til forskellige typer ejendomme: fra en lille studielejlighed til et to- eller treetagers hjem. Den ser på arbejdet af designerne og arkitekterne fra hele verden, og tager læseren med på en visuel rejse for at se de nyeste tendenser i nutidigt internationalt design i private hjem beliggende i storbyer verden over. Bogen er arrangeret i henhold til antallet af rum i hver lejlighed, eksklusiv badeværelset og køkkenet.

ROOM

PIÈCE

RAUM

KAMER

HABITACIÓN

STANZA

HABITAÇÃO

RUM

Small apartments are popular with people living alone. The residents can create their own world in just one area and bring to it their own style. To make the most of the space available screens or partitions can be used to separate the living room and the bedroom, or folding furniture can be installed, enabling the property to be adapted to generate a feeling of greater space when they are packed away.

Les appartements de dimensions réduites sont les favoris des gens qui choisissent de vivre seuls. Dans une seule pièce, on peut créer son propre univers en un seul module et lui imprimer un style personnel. Pour tirer le meilleur parti de l'espace disponible, on peut diviser la pièce à l'aide de cloisons pour séparer le salon de la chambre à coucher. On peut également utiliser des meubles escamotables pour donner plus de flexibilité et créer une sensation d'espace.

Kleine Apartments eignen sich perfekt für Menschen, die alleine leben. In einem 1-Zimmer-Apartment kann der Bewohner sich ein individuelles, einheitliches kleines Wohn-Universum einrichten. Um bestmöglich vom vorhandenen Raum zu profitieren kann das Zimmer mit Paravents oder Trennwänden eingeteilt werden, um Schlaf- und Wohnzimmer voneinander zu trennen. Eine andere Möglichkeit ist die unterschiedliche Gestaltung der Möbel; damit kann vor allem in engen Räumen ein Eindruck von Weite geschaffen werden.

Appartementen met bescheiden afmetingen zijn geliefd bij mensen die alleen wonen. In één enkele ruimte kan de bewoner zijn eigen wereld scheppen en uitdrukking geven aan zijn persoonlijke stijl. Om de ruimte optimaal te benutten kan ze met behulp van tussenschotten worden ingedeeld, zodat woon- en slaapgedeelte gescheiden zijn. Een andere mogelijkheid is het gebruik van inklapbaar meubilair. Uitgeklapt voorziet dit meubilair snel in de gewenste functie van de ruimte, ingeklapt wordt het gevoel van ruimte vergroot.

Los apartamentos de dimensiones reducidas son los preferidos por quienes deciden vivir solos. En un ambiente único, el habitante puede crear su propio universo en un solo módulo e imprimir su estilo particular. Con el objeto de aprovechar al máximo el espacio, la habitación se puede dividir con tabiques o paredes para separar la sala de estar y el dormitorio. Otra opción es montar mobiliario plegable para permitir la adaptabilidad del espacio y generar sensación de amplitud cuando se encuentran cerrados.

Chi decide di vivere da solo predilige gli appartamenti di dimensioni contenute. Chi abita in un monolocale ha la possibilità di creare un proprio universo seguendo uno stile personale. Per sfruttare al massimo lo spazio, l'abitazione può essere suddivisa con l'ausilio di schermi o tramezzi che separano zona notte e zona giorno. Un'altra opzione prevede l'utilizzo di mobili pieghevoli o a scomparsa che consentono all'ambiente di adattarsi alle esigenze e, richiudendosi, regalano una sensazione di maggiore ampiezza.

Os apartamentos pequenos gozam de popularidade entre as pessoas que moram sozinhas, que aí podem criar o seu próprio universo num espaço único que reflecte o seu estilo. Para tirar o melhor partido do espaço disponível, podem ser utilizadas telas ou divisórias para separar a sala de estar do quarto, ou recorrer ao mobiliário adaptável; dinâmico, funcional e, quando dobrado, potenciador do espaço livre.

Små lägenheter är populära bland ensamstående. Den boende kan skapa sitt eget universum på bara ett enda utrymme och förse det med sin egen stil. För att få ut det mesta möjliga av det tillgängliga utrymmet, kan skärmar eller skiljeväggar användas för att dela av vardagsrummet och sovrummet. Hopfällbara möbler kan också användas för att göra utrymmet anpassningsbart, samt för att ge en rymligare känsla när möblerna är hopfällda.

Gloucestershire Apartment

LONDON, UK

HUGH BROUGHTON ARCHITECTS

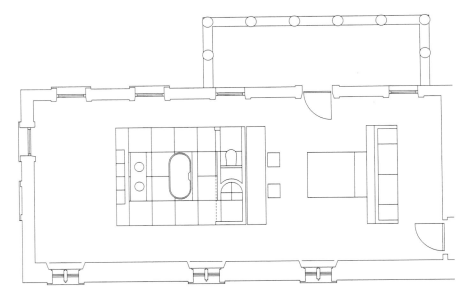

Floor plan

The project to renovate this apartment built at the beginning of the 20th century was based on joining two small rooms to create a large, continuous space. Three walls separate the bedroom from the bathroom, which is open to the communal area and contains a bath and a closed shower.

Le projet de rénovation de cet appartement du début du XXe siècle a consisté à réunir deux petites pièces et à les transformer en un seul espace continu. Trois murs séparent la chambre de la salle de bains, qui s'ouvre sur l'espace commun et est dotée d'une baignoire et d'une douche fermée.

Ziel der Renovierung dieses Anfang des 20. Jahrhunderts entstandenen Apartments war es, zwei kleine Zimmer zu verbinden und in einen durchgehenden Raum zu verwandeln. Drei Räume trennen das Schlafzimmer vom Badezimmer, welches sich zum Wohnraum hin öffnet und eine Badewanne sowie eine geschlossene Duschkabine enthält.

De renovatie van dit appartement uit het begin van de 20e eeuw had als oogmerk twee kleine kamers samen te voegen en er één doorlopende ruimte van te maken. Drie wanden grenzen de slaapkamer af van de badkamer, die open is naar de gemeenschappelijke ruimte en een badkuip en afgesloten douche heeft.

El proyecto para renovar este apartamento de principios de siglo XX se basó en unir dos pequeñas habitaciones y transformarlas en un solo espacio continuo. Tres paredes delimitan el dormitorio del cuarto de baño, que se encuentra abierto al espacio común y posee una bañera y una ducha cerrada.

Alla base del progetto di ristrutturazione di questo appartamento dell'inizio del XX secolo, l'esigenza di riunire due piccoli ambienti per creare un unico, ampio spazio. Tre pareti separano la camera da letto dal bagno, che si apre sull'area comune e contiene una vasca da bagno e una colonna doccia.

O projecto de renovação deste apartamento do início do século XX teve por base a junção de dois pequenos quartos, com vista à criação de um espaço grande e contínuo. São três as paredes que separam o quarto da casa de banho, aberta para a área comum e que contém uma banheira e um duche fechado.

Projektet med att renovera den här lägenheten som härrör från början av 1900-talet började med att två små rum förenades för att skapa ett stort, enhetligt utrymme. Tre väggar avdelar sovrummet från badrummet, med badkar och en avskild dusch, som man har tillgång till från gemensamhetsutrymmet.

Apartment 204
MIAMI, USA

ESTUDIO URIBE - PABLO URIBE

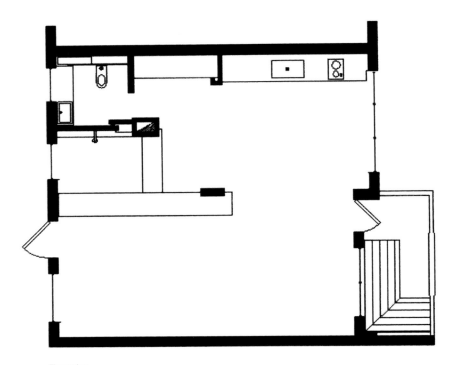

Floor plan

With the exception of the walls separating the bathroom, the space is completely open. Cement and steel are predominant, with varying shades of white on the walls and ceiling. A long bench defines the shower area, structures the space and is a multifunctional piece of furniture.

L'espace est ici complètement ouvert, à l'exception des murs qui isolent la salle de bains. Le ciment et l'acier prédominent, et les couleurs des murs et des plafonds sont des variations de blanc. Un long banc délimite l'espace de la douche, structure l'espace et fait office de meuble multifonction.

Dieser Wohnraum ist mit Ausnahme der Badezimmerwände komplett offen gestaltet. Stahlbeton und verschiedene Weißtöne an den Decken und Wänden dominieren das Erscheinungsbild. Eine lange Bank wird zum multifunktionalen Möbelstück und dient unter anderem als Begrenzung der Dusche sowie als räumliches Strukturelement.

De ruimte is volledig open op de wand die de badkamer afscheidt na. Beton en staal domineren, en op het plafond en de wanden zijn verschillende wittinten aangebracht. Een lange bank grenst de douche af, geeft structuur aan de ruimte en is tevens een multifunctioneel meubelstuk.

El espacio es totalmente abierto, a excepción de las paredes de separación del baño. Predominan el cemento y el acero, y los colores son variaciones de blanco en los techos y las paredes. Un banco alargado delimita la ducha, estructura el espacio y sirve de mueble multifuncional.

Lo spazio è completamente aperto, con l'unica eccezione delle pareti che separano il bagno. I materiali predominanti sono l'acciaio e il cemento, con varie gradazioni di bianco per pareti e soffitto. Una lunga panchina, elemento d'arredo multifunzionale, definisce l'area dedicata alla doccia e struttura lo spazio.

Excepção feita às paredes que separam a casa de banho, este é um espaço totalmente aberto. O betão e o aço predominam, em variações de branco sobre as paredes e os tectos. Um longo banco define a zona dos banhos, estrutura o espaço e constitui-se como uma peça de mobiliário multifuncional.

Med undantag av väggarna som avskiljer badrummet från resten, är utrymmet helt öppet. Cement och stål dominerar, med olika vita nyanser på väggar och tak. En lång bänk avdelar duschutrymmet, strukturerar upp utrymmet och är en möbel som har flera funktioner.

Loftcube

BERLIN, GERMANY

WERNER AISSLINGER/STUDIO AISSLINGER

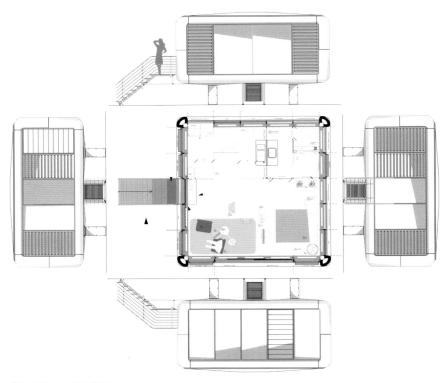

Floor plan and elevations

Aisslinger designed two versions of the Loftcube — one for a home and the other for an office, and both measuring 36 m². The concept of the project was to make use of the flat roofs of the buildings to construct temporary homes which would appeal to people of all ages and lifestyles.

Aisslinger a conçu deux versions de son Loftcube : un studio et un bureau, de 36 m² chacun. Le concept de ce projet est de tirer parti des toitures plates des immeubles pour y installer des lieux de vie temporaires, pouvant attirer des gens de tous âges et de tous styles de vie.

Aisslinger entwarf zwei Versionen des „Loftcube" mit jeweils 36 m²; eine dient als Wohnung, die andere als Büro. Der zentrale Gedanke bei dem Projekt war es, die Flachdächer der Gebäude als temporalen Wohnraum nutzen zu können – eine Idee, die Menschen jeden Alters und verschiedenster Lebensstile anspricht.

Aisslinger heeft twee versies van de Loftcube ontworpen: een voor een woning en een voor een kantoor, beide van 36 m². Het idee van het ontwerp is te profiteren van de platte daken van grote gebouwen door daar tijdelijke woningen neer te zetten – aantrekkelijk voor mensen van alle leeftijden en leefstijlen.

Aisslinger ha diseñado dos versiones de Loftcube, una para vivienda y otra para despacho, de 36 m² cada una. La idea del proyecto es aprovechar los tejados planos de los edificios para viviendas temporales, por lo que tiene un gran potencial para gente de todas edades y estilos de vida.

Aisslinger ha progettato due versioni del Loftcube: una casa e un ufficio, entrambi con un'ampiezza di 36 m². Il concetto alla base del progetto prevede l'utilizzo dei tetti piatti degli edifici per costruire abitazioni temporanee adatte a persone di tutte le età, indipendentemente dallo stile di vita.

A Aisslinger desenhou duas versões do *Loftcube* – uma para uma casa e outra para um escritório, medindo ambas 36 m². O conceito do projecto foi o de aproveitar as coberturas planas dos edifícios para construir habitações temporárias que fossem apelativas para pessoas de diferentes escalões etários e estilos de vida.

Aisslinger skapade två varianter av Loftcube – en som bostad och den andra som kontor, och båda på en 36 m² stor yta. Idén var att utnyttja byggnadernas platta tak för att skapa tillfälliga bostäder som drar till sig människor av alla åldrar och med olika livsstilar.

Miami White

MIAMI, USA

PABLO URIBE

© Pep Escoda

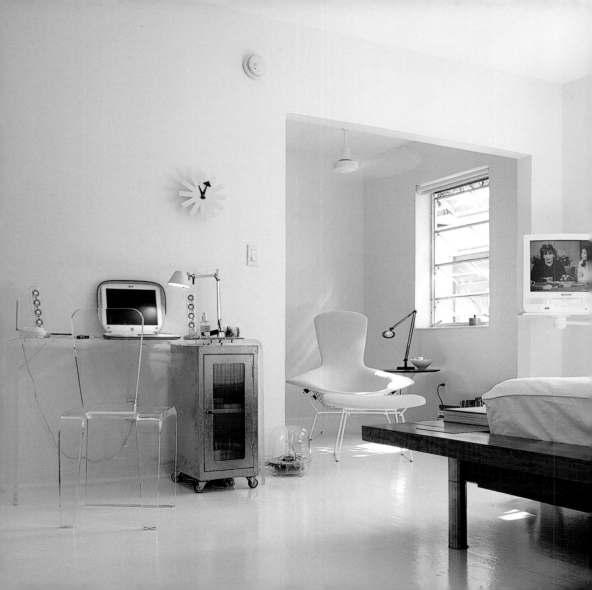

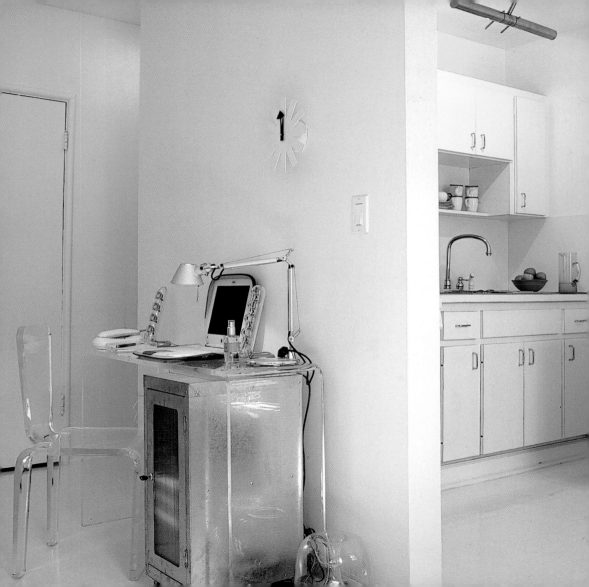

Decorated in a simple fashion with minimal furniture, this multifunctional space contains a bed which converts into a type of sofa.

Dans cet espace multifonction au mobilier minimaliste, le lit peut se transformer en un vaste sofa.

Dieser multifunktionale Raum zeichnet sich durch Nüchternheit und spärliche Möblierung aus. Das Bett kann in ein Sofa verwandelt werden.

In deze zeer sobere en alleen met het hoogst nodige meubilair ingerichte, multifunctionele ruimte doet het bed ook dienst als een soort bank.

Decorado con austeridad y un mobiliario mínimo, en este espacio multifuncional la cama se convierte también en sofá.

Questo spazio multifunzionale, arredato con austerità utilizzando mobili minimalisti, contiene un letto che si trasforma in una sorta di divano.

Decorado num estilo simples e com mobiliário minimalista, este espaço multifuncional recebe uma cama transformável numa espécie de sofá.

Det här flerfunktionella utrymmet, som har dekorerats på ett enkelt sätt med så lite möbler som möjligt, har en säng som kan förvandlas till en slags soffa.

Monolocal

MILAN, ITALY

STUDIO ASSOCIATO BETTINELLI

© Andrea Martiradonna

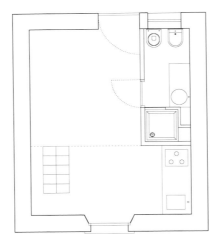

Floor plan

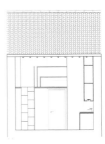

Sections

Placing the living room on two levels made the most of the small surface area in this apartment. To give a greater feeling of space, lineal shapes were chosen and white is the predominant color. It combines with the lighting to create an intimate atmosphere in the property.

La surface réduite de cet appartement a été optimisée en divisant le salon en deux niveaux. Les formes linéaires et le blanc prédominent et jouent avec la lumière pour créer une impression d'amplitude et donner une atmosphère intime à cet espace.

Die beschränkte Grundfläche dieses Apartments wurde durch die Einteilung des Wohnzimmers in zwei Ebenen erweitert. Lineare Formen und die Farbe Weiß rufen den Eindruck von Weite hervor und schaffen durch ein raffiniertes Spiel mit der Beleuchtung eine intime und heimelige Atmosphäre.

De beperkte oppervlakte van deze woning werd geoptimaliseerd door de woonkamer twee niveaus te geven. Voor een ruimtelijker gevoel werd gekozen voor strakke lijnen en de kleur wit. In een spel met het licht geven ze de woning een intieme sfeer.

La reducida superficie de este piso se optimizó mediante la división del salón en dos niveles. Para dar más sensación de amplitud se eligieron las formas lineales y el predominio del color blanco, que, al jugar con la iluminación, confieren una atmósfera intimista a la vivienda.

Le dimensioni contenute di questo appartamento sono state sfruttate al meglio distribuendo il living su due livelli. Per ampliare visivamente lo spazio si è puntato sulle forme lineari e sul bianco come colore predominante. L'illuminazione contribuisce a creare un'atmosfera intima.

A diminuta área deste apartamento foi optimizada através da divisão da zona de estar em dois níveis. No sentido de aumentar a sensação espacial, optou-se por um design de linhas rectas e pelo predomínio da cor branca. Esta, combina com a iluminação e dá à casa um ambiente de grande intimidade.

Den här lägenhetens lilla yta utnyttjades maximalt genom att vardagsrummet delades upp på två våningar. För att ge utrymmet en större känsla, valdes raka former, och den dominerande färgen blev vitt. Detta i kombination med belysningen skapar en intim atmosfär i lägenheten.

All in One

HONG KONG, CHINA

GARY CHANG/EDGE (HK) LTD

© Almond Chu

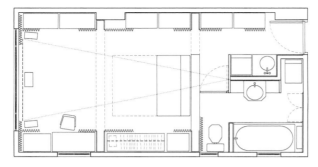

Floor plan

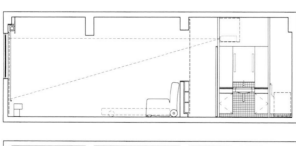

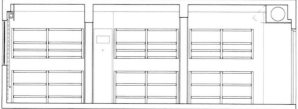

Sections

The bed can be used as a sofa, turning the bedroom into a living room and vice versa. The clothes closet and the shelves are covered by white drapes to create a feeling of luminosity.

Le lit peut servir de sofa et transformer la chambre en salon, ou vice versa. L'armoire à vêtements et les étagères sont dissimulées derrière des rideaux blancs qui donnent de la luminosité à la pièce.

Durch die Verwandlung des Bettes in ein Sofa kann das Schlaftimmer zum Wohnzimmer werden und umgekehrt. Der Kleiderschrank und die Regale werden durch weiße Vorhänge verdeckt, die dem Raum Helligkeit verleihen.

Het bed kan als bank worden gebruikt. Zo wordt van de slaapkamer een woonkamer gemaakt en omgekeerd. Voor de kledingkast en de rekken zijn witte gordijnen gehangen om een lichte sfeer te creëren.

La cama puede utilizarse como sofá, transformando el dormitorio en una sala de estar y viceversa. El armario ropero y los estantes se encuentran cubiertos por cortinas blancas para dar sensación de luminosidad.

Il letto può fungere da divano trasformando la camera da letto in soggiorno e viceversa. Armadio e scaffali sono coperti da drappi bianchi che creano una sensazione di luminosità.

A cama pode servir de sofá, transformando o quarto em sala de estar e vice-versa. Os roupeiros e as prateleiras estão cobertas por panos brancos, criando uma sensação de maior luminosidade.

Sängen kan användas som soffa, vilket förvandlar sovrummet till vardagsrum och tvärtom. Klädgarderoben och hyllorna täcks av vita draperier för att skapa en ljusare känsla.

70 > 77

Apartment on Ocean Drive
MIAMI, USA

PIERCE ALLEN - DD ALLEN

© Pep Escoda

An open plan area with no partition walls was created, with just a stately cement column in the room. The kitchen was kept as simple as possible in one corner, hidden behind the bar. The bathroom and the bed are both integrated into the space.

Ici, on a créé un espace dégagé, sans aucune cloison de séparation, avec pour seul élément structurel une colonne en ciment. La cuisine se réduit à un coin situé derrière le bar. La salle de bains et le lit sont également intégrés à cet espace.

Fehlende Trennwände erzeugen einen Eindruck von Weite und Einheitlichkeit, der lediglich durch eine geschmackvolle Säule aus Beton unterbrochen wird. Die Küchenausstattung, die sich hinter der Bar befindet, ist auf das Wesentlichste beschränkt. Badezimmer und Bett befinden sich ebenfalls in diesem einen Raum.

Deze lichtdoorlatende ruimte zonder scheidingswanden wordt alleen doorbroken door een fraaie betonnen zuil. Keukenspullen zijn tot het allernoodzakelijkste beperkt en zijn in een hoek achter de bar weggestopt. De badkamer en het bed zijn eveneens in de ruimte opgenomen.

Se creó una atmósfera diáfana sin ningún tabique se separación, intervenida tan sólo por una escultural columna de cemento. La cocina se reduce a lo más elemental en una esquina escondida detrás del bar. El baño y la cama también se encuentran integrados al espacio.

Regna un'atmosfera diafana in questo spazio a pianta aperta, privo di elementi divisori, tranne per la presenza di un'imponente colonna scultorea. La cucina, nascosta in un angolo dietro al bar, è arredata con estrema semplicità. Sia il bagno sia il letto sono integrati nello spazio.

Foi criado um espaço aberto, sem quaisquer paredes divisórias e apenas com uma imponente coluna de cimento a rasgá-lo. A cozinha manteve a sua simplicidade, aninhada a um canto por detrás do bar. A casa de banho e a cama foram também integrados neste espaço.

En yta med öppen planlösning utan skiljeväggar skapades, och det enda som bryter utrymmet är en ståtlig cementpelare. Ett mycket enkelt kök, som hålls dolt bakom baren, skapades i ena hörnet. Badrummet och sängen har båda integrerats i utrymmet.

78 [>] 87

Rue Rochechouart Apartment
PARIS, FRANCE

PETER TYBERGHIEN

© Alejandro Bahamón

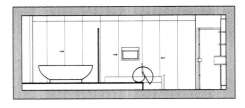

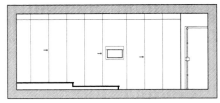

Sections

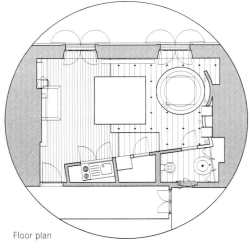

Floor plan

This compact but luxurious apartment was designed for guests on short visits to Paris. The unusual distribution includes a transparent glass screen which becomes translucent at the touch of a button and serves to separate the bed from the bath.

Cet appartement compact mais luxueux a été conçu pour accueillir des hôtes pour de courts séjours à Paris. L'organisation de l'espace est originale, et comprend un panneau en verre transparent qui devient translucide simplement en appuyant sur un bouton, et qui sépare le lit de la baignoire.

Diese luxuriöse, kompakte Wohnung wurde gestaltet, um Gäste während ihres Aufenthaltes in Paris zu beherbergen. Die originelle Gestaltung zeichnet sich unter anderem durch einen Wandschirm aus transparentem Glas aus, der auf Knopfdruck lichtundurchlässig wird. Seine Funktion ist es, das Bett vom Badezimmer abzutrennen.

Dit luxueuze, compacte appartement werd ontworpen om tijdens korte verblijven in Parijs gasten te kunnen ontvangen. Het glazen kamerscherm dat een opvallend element is in de inrichting, wordt met een druk op de knop doorzichtig en dient als scheiding tussen bed en badkuip.

Este lujoso apartamento compacto fue diseñado para albergar invitados durante estancias cortas en París. Su singular distribución incluye una mampara de vidrio transparente que se vuelve translúcida con sólo pulsar un botón, y cuya función es separar la cama de la bañera.

Questo appartamento compatto e lussuoso è stato progettato per accogliere ospiti durante le brevi visite a Parigi. L'insolita disposizione comprende uno schermo in cristallo trasparente che diventa opaco premendo un tasto e che funge da elemento divisorio tra bagno e camera da letto.

Este apartamento compacto mas luxuoso foi pensado para receber hóspedes de passagem por Paris. A sua inusitada distribuição inclui um painel em vidro transparente que se torna translúcido ao toque de um botão e separa a cama da banheira.

Den här kompakta men lyxiga lägenheten designades för gäster på korta visiter i Paris. Den ovanliga planlösningen innefattar en genomskinlig glasskärm, som blir halvgenomskinlig när man trycker på en knapp och som fungerar som skiljevägg mellan sängen och badrummet.

Domestic Curio-Box

HONG KONG, CHINA

GARY CHANG, JERRY SHE/EDGE (HK) LTD.

© Edge Design Institute

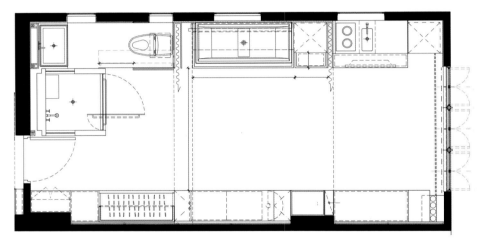

Floor plan

Using the principles of change, choice and connection, the architects designed components that are hidden away out of sight, an intelligent use of space that provides maximum comfort and efficiency in this compact apartment.

Les architectes ont recherché le changement, la possibilité de choix et la communication, et ont créé des composants qui jouent à cache-cache avec les occupants de l'appartement. C'est une façon intelligente d'optimiser l'espace et la fonctionnalité de ce logement compact.

Die Aspekte Abwechslung, Variantenreichtum sowie die Schaffung von Verbindungen standen bei der Konzeption der Wohnung im Mittelpunkt – davon zeugen beispielsweise verschiedene Elemente, die sich dem Auge des Bewohners verbergen. Dank einer intelligenten Planung wird der begrenzte Raum optimal genutzt.

Met het idee dat dingen naar keuze veranderd en op elkaar afgestemd konden worden, ontwierpen de architecten elementen die 'verstoppertje spelen' met de bewoners. Zo wordt de ruimte intelligent gebruikt en zijn het comfort en de efficiëntie van dit compacte appartement optimaal.

Con los conceptos de cambio y conectividad, los arquitectos diseñaron componentes que juegan al escondite con los habitantes del espacio, lo que constituye una forma inteligente de distribución y permite optimizar la comodidad y eficiencia de este apartamento compacto.

Seguendo i principi di mutabilità, scelta e connessione, gli architetti hanno progettato componenti nascosti alla vista e hanno fatto ricorso a un uso intelligente dello spazio per ottimizzare il confort e l'efficienza di questo appartamento compatto.

Recorrendo aos princípios de mudança, selecção e conectividade, os arquitectos desenharam componentes cuja presença no espaço fica disfarçada, num aproveitamento inteligente, confortável e eficiente da área disponível deste apartamento compacto.

Genom att använda sig av principerna om förändring, valmöjlighet och samband, skapade arkitekterna komponenter som leker kurragömma med de boende. Detta är ett intelligent sätt att använda sig av utrymmet, som ger den här kompakta lägenheten maximal komfort och effektivitet.

ROOMS

PIÈCES

RÄUME

KAMERS

HABITACIONES

STANZE

HABITACIONAIS

RUM

2

Ideal for couples with no children, one of the rooms becoming multifunctional: the living room and dining room are joined to create the main room, separate from the bedroom. Large cushions in the living area can double up as bedding on the floor for visiting guests. In the kitchen, shelves can be fitted against the wall with a folding table. In the bedroom it is advisable to install closets with sliding doors and beds with storage drawers.

Wenn eines der Zimmer multifunktional angelegt ist, eignet sich diese Wohnform perfekt für Paare ohne Kinder. Das Wohn- und das Esszimmer befinden sich einem Raum, der gleichzeitig den Mittelpunkt der Wohnung bildet. Für das Wohnzimmer empfiehlt es sich, große Kissen bereitzuhalten – so finden sich zahlreiche Sitzmöglichkeiten für Gäste. Die Küche kann mit Wandregalen und einem kleinen Tisch zum Frühstücken ausgestattet werden. Schränke mit Schiebetüren und ein Bett mit Bettkasten bieten Stauraum im Schlafzimmer.

Ideales para parejas sin niños, uno de los ambientes se transforma en multifuncional: la sala de estar y el comedor se encuentran unificados y conforman la habitación principal de la casa, separada del dormitorio. En la sala de estar se aconseja colocar almohadones, que podrán ser utilizados en el suelo para cuando el número de visitas aumenta. La cocina puede contener estantes adosados a la pared, así como también una mesa plegable tipo desayunador. En el dormitorio, lo ideal son armarios con puertas correderas y cama-cajón.

São ideais para casais sem filhos, com um dos quartos a assumir um papel multifuncional: as salas de estar e de jantar formam a divisão central da casa e estão separadas do quarto. Na sala de estar podem colocar-se almofadões que, se houver visitas, servem de cama. Na cozinha, as estantes devem estar fixas à parede e a mesa deve ser desdobrável. No quarto, aconselha-se a instalação de roupeiros com portas deslizantes e de uma cama com gavetas.

Ils sont idéaux pour les couples sans enfant. L'une des pièces fait office de salon-salle à manger. C'est la pièce principale du logement, et elle est séparée de la chambre à coucher. Il est recommandé d'y disposer des coussins de sol pour accueillir les visiteurs. La cuisine peut être dotée d'étagères adossées au mur et d'une table pliante également montée sur le mur, pour les petits-déjeuners par exemple. Dans la chambre, l'ameublement idéal se compose de placards à portes coulissantes et d'un lit à tiroir.

Ideaal voor stellen zonder kinderen. De belangrijkste kamer van het huis heeft meerdere functies, waar woon- en eetgedeelte worden ondergebracht. De slaapkamer is een apart vertrek. In de woonkamer kunnen grote kussens op de vloer worden gelegd als er veel mensen op bezoek komen. In de keuken is het raadzaam rekken of planken op te hangen en een inklapbare ontbijttafel te plaatsen. In de slaapkamer zijn kasten met schuifdeuren en een bed met laden eronder ideaal.

Questa tipologia è ideale per le coppie senza figli, poiché uno degli ambienti diventa multifunzionale: il soggiorno e la sala da pranzo s'incontrano e si fondono nel locale principale dell'abitazione, separato dalla camera da letto. Nell'area living, la collocazione di grandi cuscini sarà utile per far accomodare un numero maggiore di ospiti. La cucina può contenere un sistema di mobili a parete e un tavolo da pranzo pieghevole. In camera da letto, invece, sono perfetti gli armadi con ante scorrevoli e i letti-contenitori.

Det här är idealet för par utan barn, eftersom ett av utrymmena kan bli flerfunktionellt. Vardagsrummet och matsalen, som är avskilda från sovrummet, förenas för att fungera som bostadens huvudsakliga rum. I vardagsrummet kan man placera stora kuddar, som även kan fungera som sovunderlag när man får besök. I köket kan hyllor placeras tillsammans med ett hopfällbart bord på väggen. I sovrummet rekommenderar man att garderober med skjutdörrar och sängar med förvaringslådor används.

Made in Brazil
NEW YORK, USA

ARTHUR DE MATTOS CASAS

© Pep Escoda

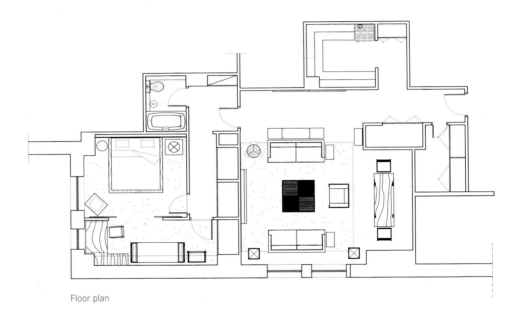

Floor plan

This property has rustic decorative elements and simple ethnic touches, with a large mirror reflecting the room and increasing the feeling of space. The dining room, the most minimalist area of the apartment, has a Japanese style.

Le décor de ce salon comporte des éléments rustiques et des objets d'inspiration ethnique. L'espace est visuellement agrandi par le très grand miroir placé sur l'un des murs. La salle à manger, la zone la plus minimaliste de l'appartement, est de style japonais.

Rustikale Dekorationselemente mit leichtem ethnischem Einschlag zeichnen diesen Raum aus – durch den großen Spiegel wird er optisch verdoppelt. Das in nüchternem japanischem Stil eingerichtete Esszimmer bildet den minimalistischsten Raum der Wohnung.

Deze ruimte met rustieke details in het interieur en enkele vleugjes exotisch minimalisme wordt weerkaatst door een grote spiegel, waardoor ze er twee keer zo groot uitziet. De sobere eetkamer in Japanse stijl is de meest minimalistische ruimte van de woning.

Con detalles decorativos rústicos y con toques de minimalismo étnico, un gran espejo proyecta el ambiente y duplica la sensación espacial. El comedor, el espacio más minimalista de la vivienda, es austero y de estilo japonés.

In questa abitazione gli elementi decorativi rustici si affiancano a tocchi etnici minimalisti, mentre un grande specchio riflette l'ambiente e amplifica l'impressione di spazio. L'austera sala da pranzo, la parte più minimalista dell'appartamento, si caratterizza per lo stile giapponese.

Esta casa apresenta elementos decorativos rústicos, com apontamentos étnicos e minimalistas. Um enorme espelho reflecte o quarto e fá-lo parecer maior. A sala de jantar, a zona mais minimalista do apartamento, é simples e de inspiração nipónica.

Den här lägenheten har rustika dekorativa inslag och en minimalistisk, etnisk touche, med en stor spegel där rummet reflekteras och som förhöjer den rymliga känslan. Matsalen, den mest minimalistiska delen i lägenheten, är enkel med en japansk stil.

Formal Unity

BOGOTÁ, COLOMBIA

GUILLERMO ARIAS, LUIS CUARTAS

© Eduardo Consuegra, Pablo Rojas, Álvaro Gutiérrez

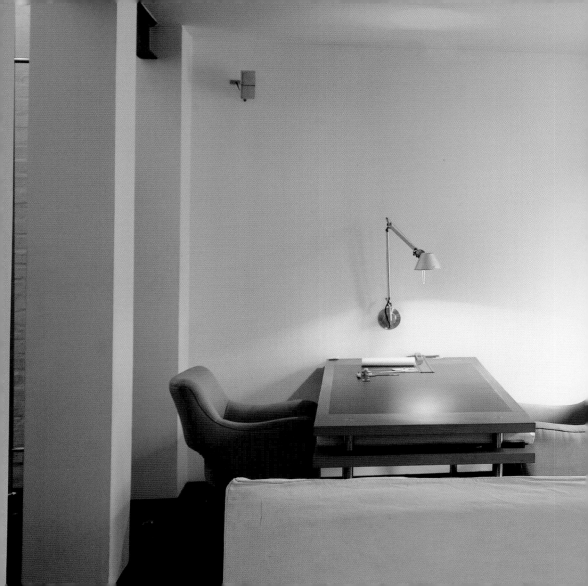

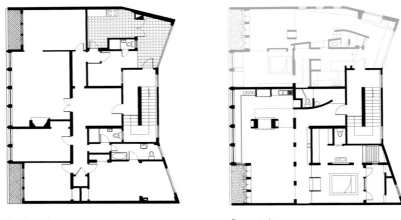

Previous plan

Present plan

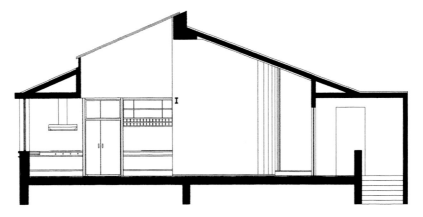

Transversal section

The bed and the window frames were designed specifically for this apartment. The old fireplace was moved into the large main room to create a partition that separates the kitchen. Wooden bookshelves cover some of the walls from floor to ceiling and occupy the spaces between the columns.

Le lit et les cadres des fenêtres ont été créés tout spécialement pour cet appartement. La cheminée ancienne a été déplacée dans la grande pièce principale afin de la séparer de la cuisine. Plusieurs étagères en bois garnies de livres couvrent certains murs du sol au plafond et occupent les espaces entre les colonnes.

Das Bett und die Fensterrahmen wurden ausschließlich für diese Wohnung designt. Der alte Kamin wurde in den Hauptwohnraum verlegt und dient nun als Trennwand zur Küche. Mehrere, vom Boden bis zur Decke reichende Bücherregale aus Holz füllen die Räume zwischen den Säulen.

Bed en raamkozijnen werden speciaal voor deze woning ontworpen. De oude schoorsteen werd naar de grote woonkamer verplaatst om die van de keuken te scheiden. Een aantal wanden heeft boekenplanken van vloer tot plafond, evenals de ruimten tussen de zuilen.

La cama y los marcos de las ventanas fueron especialmente diseñados para este piso. La vieja chimenea se trasladó a la gran sala principal para crear una separación con la cocina. Varios estantes de madera con libros cubren algunas paredes desde el suelo hasta el techo y ocupan los espacios entre las columnas.

Il letto e i telai delle finestre sono stati progettati appositamente per questo appartamento. Il vecchio caminetto è stato spostato nella grande sala principale per separare l'ambiente dalla cucina. Gli scaffali in legno a tutta altezza rivestono alcune pareti e occupano gli spazi tra le colonne.

A estrutura da cama e das janelas foi especificamente desenhada para este apartamento. A antiga lareira foi transferida para o enorme quarto principal, que assim se vê separado da cozinha. Estantes em madeira revestem algumas paredes de alto a baixo e preenchem os espaços entre colunas.

Sängen och fönsterkarmarna designades specifikt för den här lägenheten. Den gamla öppna spisen flyttades till det stora rummet för att skapa en skiljevägg som avskiljer köket. Bokhyllor i trä täcker några av väggarna från golv till tak och upptar utrymmena mellan pelarna.

Divina Morada
LONDON, UK

JONATHAN CLARK ARCHITECTS

© Jonathan Clark Architects

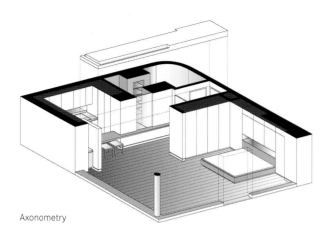

Axonometry

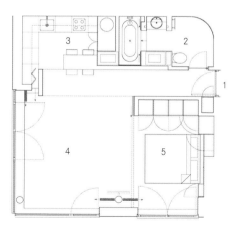

1. Entry
2. Bathroom
3. Kitchen
4. Living room
5. Bedroom

Floor plan

Located in the upper part of a converted church in Notting Hill, this space has been transformed to create an elegant attic. 'Floating' ceiling platforms and elevated panels with lighting between them were designed to give a greater feeling of height and space.

Cet espace se trouve dans la partie supérieure d'une église reconvertie de Notting Hill, et a été transformé en un attique élégant. Les plateformes flottantes du plafond et les panneaux surélevés dont les interstices abritent un système d'éclairage ont été conçus pour créer une impression de hauteur et de volume.

Diese unter dem Dach einer umgewandelten Kirche in Notting Hill gelegene Wohnung wurde zu einer eleganten Mansardenwohnung. Schwebende Deckenelemente und beleuchtete Paneele lassen einen Eindruck von Höhe und Weite entstehen.

Deze stijlvolle zolderwoning bevindt zich boven in een verbouwde kerk in Notting Hill. Zwevende plafondpanelen met verlichting in de tussenruimten werden speciaal ontworpen om een gevoel van hoogte en ruimte te creëren.

Ubicado en la parte superior de una antigua iglesia en Notting Hill, este espacio fue transformado en un elegante ático. Se diseñaron plataformas flotantes de techo y paneles elevados con iluminación en los intersticios para aumentar la sensación de altura y volumen.

Questo spazio, che si trova nella parte superiore di una chiesa sconsacrata di Notting Hill, è stato trasformato in un attico elegante. Piattaforme sospese al soffitto e pannelli sopraelevati con la luce che penetra attraverso gli interstizi concorrono ad amplificare la sensazione di altezza e di spazio.

Localizado no piso superior de uma antiga igreja de Notting Hill, este espaço foi transformado num elegante sótão. Os tectos falsos com iluminação embutida foram desenhados para aumentar a sensação de altura e de espaço.

I den övre delen av en ombyggd kyrka i Notting Hill, ligger det här utrymmet som har förändrats för att kunna skapa ett elegant loft. "Svävande" plattformer som tak och upphöjda paneler med belysning däremellan skapades för att få en känsla av mer höjd och utrymme.

Metropolitan Chic
SHANGHAI, CHINA

MOHEN DESIGN INTERNATIONAL

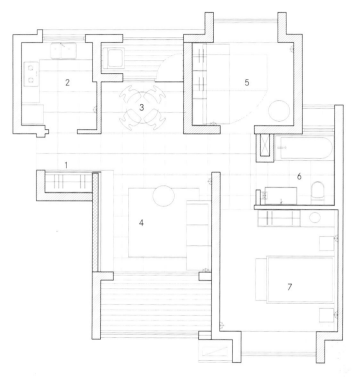

Floor plan

1. Entry
2. Kitchen
3. Dining room
4. Living room
5. Master Bedroom
6. Bathroom
7. Guest room/Study

The entrance area divides the space in two, with the kitchen and the master bedroom on one side and the social area and guest room / study on the other. The decoration is minimal, opting for visual effects created by lines, irregular surfaces and lighting.

L'entrée divise l'espace en deux parties, avec la cuisine et la chambre principale à l'opposé du salon et de la chambre d'amis/bureau. Les éléments décoratifs sont peu nombreux, car on a privilégié les effets visuels créés par les lignes, les surfaces irrégulières et l'éclairage.

Durch den Flur werden Küche und Schlafzimmer von dem am anderen Ende der Wohnung gelegenen Bereich getrennt, der Wohn- und Gästezimmer enthält. Bei der Dekoration beschränkte man sich auf das Wesentliche, wobei mithilfe von Linien, unregelmäßigen Oberflächen und Beleuchtung besondere visuelle Effekte geschaffen wurden.

De hal verdeelt de ruimte in tweeën. Keuken en hoofdslaapkamer bevinden zich tegenover de gemeenschappelijke ruimte en de logeerkamer annex studeerkamer. De inrichting werd tot een minimum beperkt om met lijnen, onregelmatige oppervlakken en verlichting visuele effecten tot stand te brengen.

El recibidor divide el espacio en dos ubicando la cocina y el dormitorio principal en el extremo opuesto del área social y el cuarto de invitados/estudio. La decoración se redujo al mínimo, optando por los efectos visuales logrados a partir de líneas y superficies irregulares y la iluminación.

L'ingresso divide in due lo spazio: da una parte la cucina e la camera padronale, dall'altra l'ambiente dedicato al ricevimento e lo studio/camera per gli ospiti. Si è scelto uno stile minimalista che privilegia gli effetti visivi creati da linee, superfici irregolari e illuminazione.

A zona de entrada divide o espaço em dois, com a cozinha e o quarto principal de um lado e com a área social e o quarto das visitas/estúdio do outro. A decoração é minimalista, apostando em efeitos visuais assentes em linhas, superfícies irregulares e numa iluminação invulgar.

Utrymmet vid ingången delar upp utrymmet i två delar, med ett kök och sovrum på ena sidan, och vardagsrum samt gästrum / arbetsrum på den andra. Dekorationen är minimal, med visuella effekter som skapas av linjer, ojämna ytor och belysning.

Light Apartment
MIAMI, USA

ANDREA MECOTTI

© Pep Escoda

A cozy, open-plan atmosphere was created with the use of white, beige and pastel colors. A light white curtain separates the living room from the dining room when necessary. The decoration is minimalist and in the bedroom the mattress has been placed on a wooden platform.

Le blanc, le beige et les couleurs pastel donnent à cet appartement une atmosphère légère et chaleureuse. Un voile blanc isole à volonté la salle à manger. Dans la chambre, la décoration est minimaliste. Le matelas repose directement sur un socle en bois.

Durch die weißen, beigen und pastellfarbenen Töne entsteht eine transparente und gleichzeitig behagliche Atmosphäre. Mit dem leichten weißen Vorhang kann das Esszimmer vom Rest des Raumes abgetrennt werden. Die Dekoration ist minimalistisch gehalten. Das Bett besteht aus einer Matratze, die direkt auf einer Holzplatte liegt.

Dankzij pastelkleuren en wit en beige werd een behaaglijke, lichte sfeer geschapen. Met een dun wit gordijn kan naar wens de eetkamer worden afgeschermd. In de slaapkamer met minimalistische inrichting ligt een groot kussen op een houten verhoging.

Gracias al blanco, al *beige* y a los colores pastel se creó una atmósfera diáfana y acogedora. Una ligera cortina blanca separa a voluntad la sala del comedor. Con una decoración minimalista, en el dormitorio, el colchón descansa directamente sobre el tablero de madera.

Il ricorso ai toni del bianco e del beige e ai colori pastello conferisce a questo appartamento un'atmosfera aperta e accogliente. All'occorrenza, una leggera tenda bianca separa la zona living dalla sala da pranzo. La decorazione segue uno stile minimalista e, in camera da letto, il materasso poggia su una piattaforma in legno.

O recurso ao branco, ao bege e aos tons de pastel contribuem para o ambiente acolhedor deste espaço aberto. Uma leve cortina branca separa, quando necessário, as salas de estar e de jantar. A decoração é minimalista, com o colchão do quarto a assentar numa plataforma de madeira.

En mysig, öppen atmosfär skapades genom användandet av vitt, beige och pastellfärger. En ljus, vit gardin gör det möjligt att dela av vardagsrummet från matsalen när det behövs. Dekorationen är minimalistisk och i sovrummet har madrassen placerats på en plattform i trä.

150 ^{> 157}

Light on White
BARCELONA, SPAIN

CRISTINA ALGÁS, PATRICIO MARTÍNEZ

© José Luis Hausmann

The bathroom connects the bedroom and the rest of the apartment. It is surrounded by sliding doors which allow access from the different rooms. The decoration is simple, comfortable and functional.

La salle de bains relie la chambre aux autres pièces de l'appartement. Elle est flanquée de deux portes coulissantes qui y donnent accès à partir des différentes pièces. La décoration est simple, confortable et fonctionnelle.

Das Badezimmer dient als Verbindung zwischen dem Schlafzimmer und den restlichen Räumen der Wohnung. Es kann über Schiebetüren von verschiedenen Bereichen der Wohnung aus betreten werden, die sich durch eine schlichte, komfortable und funktionelle Einrichtung auszeichnet.

De badkamer vormt de verbinding tussen de slaapkamer en de overige kamers van het huis. Rond de badkamer zijn schuifdeuren aangebracht, zodat hij vanuit de verschillende vertrekken te betreden is. De inrichting is eenvoudig, comfortabel en functioneel.

El cuarto de baño es el conector entre el dormitorio y el resto de las habitaciones de la casa. El baño está flanqueado por puertas correderas, que permiten acceder a él desde los distintos ambientes. La decoración es simple, confortable y funcional.

Il bagno funge da collegamento tra la camera da letto e il resto dell'appartamento. La presenza di diverse porte scorrevoli consente l'accesso da più ambienti. L'arredo è semplice, confortevole e funzionale.

A casa de banho liga o quarto ao restante apartamento. Está rodeada de portas deslizantes que permitem aceder-lhe a partir das diferentes divisões da casa. A decoração é simples, confortável e funcional.

Badrummet binder samman sovrummet med resten av lägenheten. Det omges av skjutdörrar som ger tillträde från de olika rummen. Dekorationen är enkel, bekväm och funktionell.

Walking on Air
TURIN, ITALY

UDA

© Emilio Conti

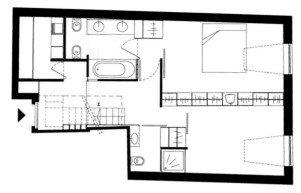

First floor plan

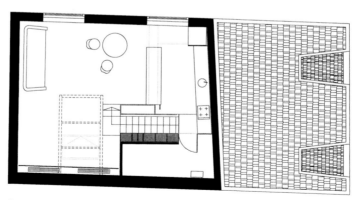

Second floor plan

A two-storey apartment, the upper level was designed like an attic to house the dining room and the living room. Use was made of the irregular-shaped ceiling to build a bookcase into the wall.

Dans cet appartement distribué sur deux niveaux, la partie supérieure a été conçue comme un attique, et abrite la salle à manger et la pièce à vivre. On a tiré parti de la ligne irrégulière du plafond pour encastrer une bibliothèque dans l'un des murs.

Das obere Stockwerk der auf zwei Ebenen verteilten Wohnung, welches das Ess- und das Wohnzimmer enthält, wirkt wie eine Mansarde. Eine der unregelmäßig geformten Dachschräge bietet den optimalen Raum für eine Bibliothek.

Dit appartement werd in twee niveaus verdeeld, waarbij het bovenste is ingericht als een loft met eetkamer en woonkamer. Er is gebruikgemaakt van de onregelmatige vorm van het plafond door boven een van de wanden een bibliotheek in te bouwen.

Distribuido en dos niveles, la parte superior de este apartamento fue diseñada como si fuera un ático, que contiene el comedor y la sala de estar. Aprovechando la irregularidad del techo, sobre una de las paredes se empotró una biblioteca.

In questo appartamento distribuito su due piani, il piano superiore è progettato come un attico per accogliere sala da pranzo e soggiorno. L'irregolarità del soffitto ha permesso di costruire una libreria incassata nella parete.

Neste apartamento de dois pisos o andar de cima foi pensado para funcionar como sótão e para receber as salas de jantar e de estar. Tirou-se partido da forma irregular do tecto para encastrar na parede uma grande estante.

I den här tvåvåningslägenheten designades den översta våningen som ett loft för att rymma matsalen och vardagsrummet. Man tog vara på det oregelbundet formade taket för att bygga en bokhylla i väggen.

Get Layered

LONDON, UK

HUGH BROUGHTON ARCHITECTS

© Carlos Domínguez

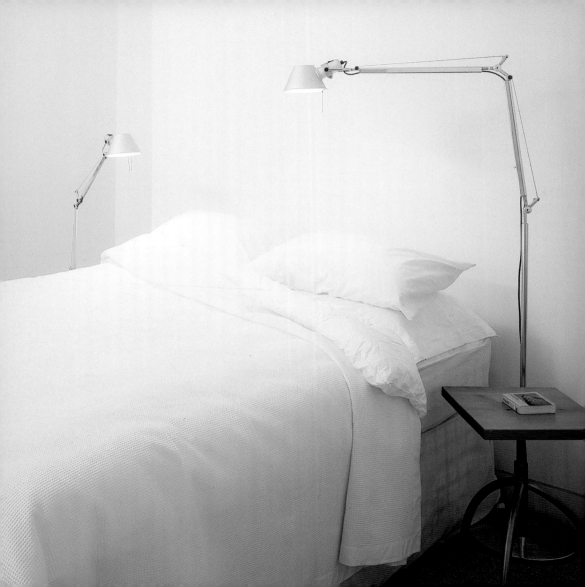

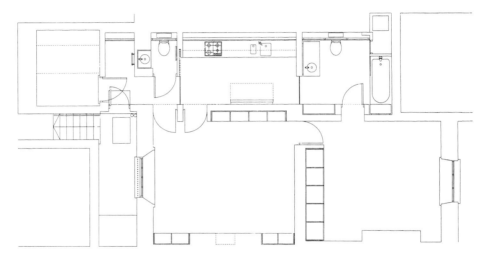

Floor plan

To create a feeling of greater space, two glass doors connect the kitchen with the living room and dining room. A folding table in the kitchen makes the space versatile.

Deux portes en verre font communiquer la pièce à vivre et la salle à manger et renforcent l'impression d'espace. La cuisine est dotée d'une table pliante qui lui donne de la flexibilité.

Um den Räumlichkeiten die größtmögliche Weite zu geben, dienen zwei Glastüren als Verbindungselemente zwischen Küche, Ess- und Wohnzimmer. Durch den Klapptisch in der Küche ist für Flexibilität gesorgt.

Om het ruimtelijke gevoel van de vertrekken te vergroten, zijn de deuren tussen de keuken en de woon- en eetkamer van glas. Dankzij de inklapbare tafel kan met de ruimte in de keuken worden gespeeld.

Para lograr sensación de mayor amplitud entre los ambientes, dos puertas de vidrios conectan la cocina con la sala de estar y el comedor. Una mesa plegable en la cocina da versatilidad al espacio.

Per creare una sensazione di maggiore ampiezza, due porte di vetro collegano la cucina al soggiorno e alla sala da pranzo. Il tavolo pieghevole scelto per la cucina rende l'ambiente versatile.

Com o intuito de aumentar a sensação espacial, foram instaladas duas portas em vidro na ligação entre a cozinha e as salas de estar e de jantar. A mesa desdobrável da cozinha traz versatilidade a este espaço.

För att skapa en känsla av ett större utrymme, binder två glasdörrar samman köket med vardagsrummet och matsalen. Ett utfällbart bord i köket gör utrymmet flexibelt.

Away from the Bustle
MIAMI, USA

O'NEILL ESPINAL + RAÚL FRONTAL

© Pep Escoda

In this Miami apartment the decoration is based on the contrast between the white walls and the dark brown floor. The furnishings and decorative elements also reflect this chromatic combination.

Dans cet appartement de Miami, la décoration est basée sur le contraste entre le blanc des murs et le marron intense du sol. Le mobilier et les détails de la décoration sont également organisés autour de cette combinaison chromatique.

Der Kontrast zwischen dem Weiß der Wände und dem intensiven Braun des Bodens geben dieser in Miami gelegenen Wohnung seine besondere Note. Diese Zweifarbigkeit bildet die Basis für Mobiliar und die Dekorationselemente.

In dit appartement in Miami vormt het contrast tussen de witte wanden en de donkerbruine vloer de basis van de inrichting. Ook het meubilair en de andere inrichtingselementen zijn afgestemd op deze kleurencombinatie.

En este apartamento de Miami, la decoración se basó en el contraste entre el blanco de las paredes y el marrón oscuro del suelo. El mobiliario y los detalles decorativos también se organizan de acuerdo con esta combinación cromática.

In questo appartamento di Miami la decorazione si basa sul contrasto tra il bianco delle pareti e il marrone scuro del pavimento. Anche gli arredi e gli elementi decorativi riflettono questa combinazione cromatica.

Neste apartamento de Miami a decoração assenta no contraste estabelecido entre o branco das paredes e o castanho-escuro do pavimento. O mobiliário e os elementos decorativos reflectem também esta combinação cromática.

I den här lägenheten i Miami har dekorationen baserats på kontrasten mellan de vita väggarna och det mörkt bruna golvet. Möblerna och de dekorativa inslagen reflekterar också den här färgkombinationen.

Micro Miracle
GREENWICH VILLAGE, NY, USA

CCS ARCHITECTURE

© Javier Haddad Conde

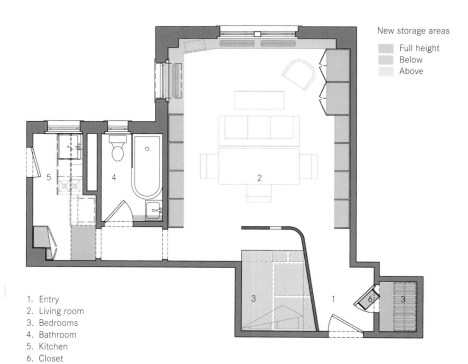

New storage areas

■ Full height
■ Below
■ Above

1. Entry
2. Living room
3. Bedrooms
4. Bathroom
5. Kitchen
6. Closet

Floor plan

This space was transformed to create a bedroom and plenty of storage space, with a casual, modern look. A micro-bedroom has been installed in what used to be the dressing room, with a queen-sized bed that has storage space underneath.

Cet espace a été transformé pour créer une chambre originale et moderne avec beaucoup d'espaces de rangement. Un grand lit placé en hauteur est dissimulé derrière une cloison arrondie, à la place de l'ancien dressing.

Dieser Raum wurde in ein lässig-modern wirkendes Schlafzimmer umgewandelt, wobei vor allem darauf geachtet wurde, reichlich Stauraum zur Verfügung zu stellen. Das vormalige Ankleidezimmer wurde zum Minischlafzimmer und enthält ein Queen-Size-Bett mit großzügigem Bettkasten.

Deze ruimte werd opgeknapt om een slaapkamer te creëren met een vlotte, moderne uitstraling en de nodige bergruimte. Van een voormalige kleedkamer werd een piepkleine slaapkamer gemaakt met een *queensize* bed met bergruimte eronder.

Este espacio se transformó para crear un dormitorio y una gran área de almacenamiento, y asimismo darle un aspecto casual y moderno. En lo que antes era un vestidor se creó un microdormitorio con una cama tamaño *queen* y espacio de almacenamiento debajo.

Questo spazio dall'aspetto casual e moderno è stato trasformato per creare una camera da letto e moltiplicare gli elementi contenitivi. Nello spazio destinato in precedenza allo spogliatoio è stata creata una micro camera da letto con letto matrimoniale dotato di base contenitore.

Este espaço foi transformado com vista à criação de um quarto e de muito espaço de arrumos, num estilo descontraído e moderno. Um mini-quarto foi instalado na antiga zona de vestir, onde uma cama de casal oferece, sob o colchão, espaço para arrumos.

Det här utrymmet förvandlades för att skapa ett sovrum och stora förvaringsutrymmen, med en ledig, modern prägel. Ett pyttelitet sovrum finns där det tidigare omklädningsrummet låg, med en säng i storlek "queen size" som har förvaringsmöjligheter undertill.

202 > 211

Capital Delight
MADRID, SPAIN

PABLO PANIAGUA

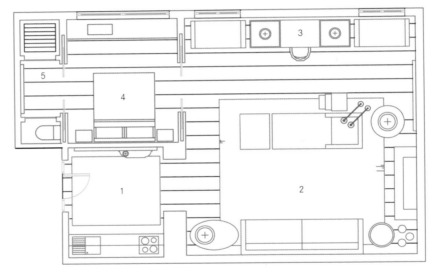

Floor plan

1. Entrance/kitchen/dining room
2. Living room
3. Study
4. Bedrooms
5. Bathroom

In this small, luxurious urban apartment the entrance area serves the purpose of hall, kitchen and dining room. The main space in the property is the living room, where people can gather round the fireplace or work in the library area.

Dans ce luxueux petit appartement citadin, l'entrée fait office de vestibule, de cuisine et de salle à manger. L'espace principal de ce logement est le salon, où l'on peut se réunir autour de la cheminée ou travailler près de la bibliothèque.

In diesem kleinen Luxusapartment fungiert der Eingangsbereich als Flur, Küche und Esszimmer. Den Mittelpunkt der Wohnung bildet das Wohnzimmer, wo der Kamin als gemütlicher Treffpunkt dient und der Bibliotheksbereich einen angenehmen Arbeitsplatz bildet.

In dit kleine, luxueuze stadsappartement heeft de entreezone zowel de functie van hal als van keuken en eetkamer. De belangrijkste ruimte van de woning is de zitkamer, waar men bij de haard kan zitten of in het bibliotheekgedeelte kan werken.

En este pequeño piso urbano de lujo la entrada funciona a la vez como recibidor, cocina y comedor. El espacio principal de la casa es el salón, donde es posible reunirse en torno a la chimenea o trabajar en el área de la biblioteca.

Questo appartamento urbano piccolo e lussuoso riserva all'ingresso la triplice funzione di locale d'accoglienza, cucina e sala da pranzo. Lo spazio principale dell'abitazione è il soggiorno: ci si può radunare intorno al camino o lavorare nell'area dedicata alla biblioteca.

Neste pequeno e luxuoso apartamento, a zona de entrada alberga o hall, a cozinha e sala de jantar. O principal espaço da casa é a sala de estar, onde os moradores se podem juntar em volta da lareira ou trabalhar na zona da biblioteca.

I den här lilla, lyxiga urbana lägenheten, fungerar utrymmet vid ingången som hall, kök och matsal. Det huvudsakliga utrymmet i lägenheten är vardagsrummet, där människor kan samlas runt den öppna spisen eller arbeta i biblioteksutrymmet.

Oriental Style
SHAM TSENG, HONG KONG, CHINA

P TANG STUDIO LTD

© Ulso Tsang

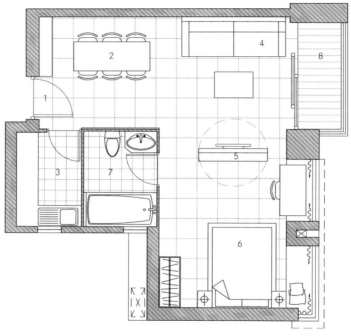

Floor plan

1. Entry
2. Dining room
3. Kitchen
4. Living room
5. Revolving Cabinet
6. Bedrooms
7. Bathroom
8. Balcony

Dark tones have been used to create a clear separation between the night-time area and the rest of the space. Other design 'tricks', such as the use of white walls and tiles, help to make this 58 m^2 apartment seem larger.

Les couleurs sombres séparent clairement la zone de nuit du reste de l'appartement. D'autres astuces d'architecture d'intérieur, comme l'utilisation des cloisons et les carreaux blancs, agrandissent visuellement cet espace de 58 m^2.

Dunkle Farbtöne grenzen den Schlafbereich klar vom Rest der Wohnung ab. Andere gestalterische Tricks, so zum Beispiel weiße Wände und Fliesen, lassen die 58 m^2 große Wohnung geräumiger erscheinen.

De zone voor de nacht is door haar donkere kleuren duidelijk gescheiden van de rest van de ruimte. Andere 'ontwerptrucs' zoals het gebruik van witte muren en witte tegels zorgen ervoor dat deze ruimte van 58 m^2 groter lijkt dan ze is.

La zona de noche se separa claramente del resto del espacio por sus tonos oscuros. Otros «trucos» de diseño tales como el uso de paredes y azulejos blancos ayudan a que este espacio de 58 m^2 parezca mayor.

La zona notte si distingue nettamente dal resto dell'ambiente per i suoi toni scuri. Grazie ad altri "accorgimenti", come l'utilizzo di pareti e piastrelle bianche, l'appartamento di 58 m^2 dà l'impressione di essere più ampio.

Recorreu-se aos tons escuros para separar de forma clara as áreas privadas da casa das suas áreas sociais. Outros "truques" do design, como o branco das paredes e a aplicação de ladrilhos, ajudam a dar dimensão a este apartamento de apenas 58 m^2.

Mörka toner har används för att klart avgränsa sovutrymmen från resten av utrymmet. Andra designknep, som till exempel användandet av vita väggar och kakel, hjälper till att få den här 58 m^2 stora lägenheten att se större ut.

Timber House

TOKYO, JAPAN

MAKIKO TSUKADA

© Mitsumasa Fujitsuka

Sheer Elegance

ROME, ITALY

FILIPPO BOMBACE

© Luigi Filetici

Loft in Plaza Mayor

MADRID, SPAIN

MANUEL OCAÑA DEL VALLE

© Alfonso Postigo

The project consisted of renovating an irregular-shaped property in an old building in the centre of Madrid to create a modern apartment. The dark wood flooring was kept and furnishings in light colors were chosen to provide a contrast and add brightness.

Le projet a consisté à rénover cet appartement irrégulier d'un vieil immeuble du centre de Madrid pour le transformer en logement moderne. Le sol en bois a été conservé, et l'on a choisi des meubles clairs pour créer un contraste et apporter de la luminosité.

Das Ziel dieses Projekts bestand darin, diese unregelmäßig geschnittene Wohnung in einem alten, im Zentrum Madrids gelegenen Gebäude in einen modernen Wohnraum zu verwandeln. Der Holzfußboden wurde erhalten und mit hellen Möbeln ergänzt, wodurch interessante Kontraste sowie optimale Lichtverhältnisse geschaffen wurden.

Het ontwerp moest van dit rommelig ingedeelde appartement in een oud gebouw in het centrum van Madrid een moderne woning maken. De vloer van donker hout bleef bewaard. Er werd voor meubilair in lichte tinten gekozen om contrast en lichtheid te creëren.

El proyecto consistió en reformar este irregular apartamento de un viejo edificio del centro de Madrid para transformarlo en un piso moderno. Se conservó el suelo de madera oscura y se eligió un mobiliario en tonos claros para crear contraste y obtener luminosidad.

Il progetto si proponeva di ristrutturare questo appartamento di pianta irregolare in un vecchio stabile al centro di Madrid per trasformarlo in un alloggio moderno. Si è scelto di mantenere il pavimento in legno scuro e di arredare l'appartamento con mobili dai toni chiari per creare un contrasto e renderlo più luminoso.

O projecto consistiu na renovação de uma casa de formas irregulares num velho edifício do centro de Madrid, com vista à criação de um apartamento moderno. Os pavimentos em madeira escura foram mantidos, optando-se por mobílias brancas para estabelecer contrastes e aumentar a luminosidade.

Projektet bestod i att renovera en oregelbundet formad lägenhet i en gammal byggnad i Madrids centrum, för att skapa en modern lägenhet. Det mörka trägolvet bevarades och möbler i ljusa färger valdes för att skapa en kontrast och ge mer ljus.

Eric's Apartment

MIAMI, USA

LUIS CASAÑAS

This 350 m² apartment has a big terrace adjoining the living room, accessible through two large sliding doors. An enormous mirror reflects the city, creating the effect of a large painting or window. The bedroom also opens onto the terrace.

Dans cet appartement de 350 m², la grande terrasse communique directement avec le salon grâce à deux portes coulissantes. L'énorme miroir reflète la ville et ressemble à un grand tableau, ou à une fenêtre. Le salon et la chambre s'ouvrent sur la terrasse.

In dieser 350 m² großen Wohnung betritt man vom Wohnzimmer aus über zwei riesige Schiebetüren eine großzügige Terrasse. Der enorme Spiegel, der die Stadt reflektiert, wirkt wie ein großes Gemälde oder ein Fenster. Das Wohn- und das Schlafzimmer öffnen sich zur Terrasse hin.

In dit appartement van 350 m² staat het ruime terras via twee grote schuifdeuren rechtstreeks in verbinding met de woonkamer. De reusachtige spiegel weerkaatst de stad en lijkt net een groot schilderij of raam. Het terras is zowel vanuit de woonkamer als vanuit de slaapkamer toegankelijk.

En este apartamento de 350 m² la amplia terraza se comunica directamente con el salón a través de dos grandes puertas correderas. El enorme espejo refleja la ciudad y crea el efecto de una gran pintura o ventana. El salón y el dormitorio se abren a la terraza.

In questo appartamento di 350 m² l'ampia terrazza comunica direttamente con il salone per mezzo di due grandi porte scorrevoli. Uno specchio enorme riflette la città, dando l'impressione di trovarsi di fronte a un grande quadro o a una finestra. Anche la camera da letto si affaccia sulla terrazza.

Este apartamento de 350 m² apresenta, junto à sala, um grande terraço, acessível através de duas portas deslizantes. Um enorme espelho reflecte a cidade, confundindo-se com uma pintura ou até com uma janela. O quarto abre também para o terraço.

Intill vardagsrummet i den här 350 m² stora lägenheten finns en stor terrass, som nås genom två stora skjutdörrar. Staden reflekteras i en enorm spegel, som ser ut som en stor tavla eller ett fönster. Sovrummet öppnar också upp till terrassen.

Steve Apartment
MILAN, ITALY

MARCO SAVORELLI

© Matteo Piazza

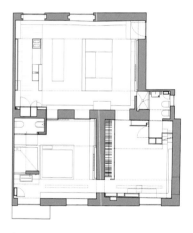

Floor plan

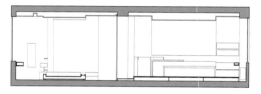

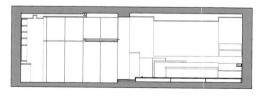

Sections

The living room, the dining room and the kitchen — which is discreetly hidden behind a medium-height partition — are located in the central area of the apartment. Dark wood and the color white dominate and the design is based on the principles of *feng shui*.

Le salon, la salle à manger et la cuisine, discrètement dissimulées derrière une demi-cloison, occupent la zone centrale de l'appartement. La décoration, où prédominent le blanc et le bois sombre, se base sur les principes du feng shui.

Wohnzimmer, Küche und Esszimmer — alle drei Räume sind hinter einer halbhohen Abtrennung versteckt — bilden den zentralen Bereich dieser Wohnung. Neben dem Prinzip des Feng Shui dominieren die Farbe Weiß und dunkles Holz das gesamte Design.

Woonkamer, eetkamer en keuken — die onopvallend achter een halve afscheiding schuilgaan — beslaan het centrale gedeelte van dit appartement. In deze inrichting, die gebaseerd is op de principes van feng shui, domineren de kleur wit en het donkere hout.

La sala de estar, el comedor y la cocina, que discretamente se ocultan detrás de una media partición, ocupan el área central del apartamento. Bajo el predominio total del color blanco y la madera oscura, el diseño está basado en los principios del *feng shui*.

La parte centrale dell'appartamento è occupata dal soggiorno, dalla sala da pranzo e dalla cucina, nascoste in modo discreto da un tramezzo di altezza media. Il design, in cui predominano il colore bianco e il legno scuro, si basa sui principi del feng shui.

As salas de estar e de jantar, bem como a cozinha — discretamente escondida por trás de uma divisória a meia altura — situam-se na zona central do apartamento. As madeiras escuras e o branco dominam o espaço, e o design baseia-se nos princípios do *feng shui*.

Vardagsrummet, matsalen och köket — som har dolts diskret bakom en skiljevägg av medelhöjd — ligger i lägenhetens centrala utrymme. Mörkt trä och vitt dominerar och designen grundar sig i *feng shui*.

Contemporary Beginnings

ROME, ITALY

FILIPPO BOMBACE

Juan Carlos Arcila-Duque Residence
MIAMI, USA

JUAN CARLOS ARCILA-DUQUE

© Pep Escoda

The architect of this apartment also lives here and so it has been adapted to meet his needs: plenty of space to house his collection of photographs and *objets d'art*. The majority of the furnishings were also designed by Juan Carlos Arcila-Duque.

L'architecte de cet appartement est également son occupant, il l'a donc adapté à ses besoins personnels : un espace pour accueillir sa collection de photographies et d'objets d'arts. La majeure partie du mobilier a également été conçue par Juan Carlos Arcila-Duque.

Der Architekt, der in dieser Wohnung lebt, hat diese seinen persönlichen Bedürfnissen angepasst: sie verfügt vor allem über genügend Platz für seine Foto- und Kunstsammlung. Juan Carlos Arcila-Duque hat außerdem die Einrichtung entworfen.

Bewoner van dit appartement is de architect zelf, die het aan zijn persoonlijke behoeften aanpaste. Hij wilde voldoende ruimte hebben voor zijn collectie foto's en kunstvoorwerpen. Ook het meeste meubilair ontwierp Juan Carlos Arcila-Duque zelf.

El propio arquitecto es el morador de este apartamento, que lo adaptó a sus necesidades personales: disponer de un gran espacio para albergar su colección de fotografías y objetos de arte. La mayoría del mobiliario también ha sido diseñado por Juan Carlos Arcila-Duque.

L'architetto ha adattato quest'appartamento, che è anche la sua residenza, alle sue esigenze personali: disporre di uno spazio sufficiente per la sua collezione di fotografie e di oggetti d'arte. Anche la maggior parte dei mobili è stata progettata da Juan Carlos Arcila-Duque.

O arquitecto que desenhou este apartamento é o seu ocupante, pelo que ponderou cuidadosamente as suas próprias necessidades: muito espaço para acolher a sua colecção de fotografias e *objets d'art*. Grande parte do mobiliário foi também desenhado por Juan Carlos Arcila-Duque.

Arkitekten som skapade byggnaden bor också här, och därför har den anpassats efter hans behov: stora utrymmen för att förvara hans fotosamling och konstobjekt. Majoriteten av hans möbler har även designats av Juan Carlos Arcila-Duque.

Apartment in South Beach
MIAMI, USA

LUIS CASAÑAS

© José Luis Hausmann (Stylist: Jorge Rangel)

The entrance comes straight into the open living room which leads to the terrace. The glass façade affords a spectacular view of South Beach, Florida. The kitchen is separate although it has no door: it is small and practical and also serves as a bar.

À partir de l'entrée, on arrive directement dans le salon ouvert puis sur la terrasse. La façade en verre donne une vue spectaculaire sur South Beach, en Floride. La cuisine est séparée du reste de l'appartement bien qu'elle n'ait pas de porte. Elle est très petite et très pratique, et fait également office de bar.

Vom Eingangsbereich dieser Wohnung gelangt man direkt in das offene Wohnzimmer – dieses wiederum ermöglicht den Zugang zur Terrasse. Die verglaste Fassade bietet eine spektakuläre Aussicht auf South Beach, Florida. Die Küche bildet trotz fehlender Tür einen separaten Raum: Sie ist klein, praktisch und dient als Bar.

Vanuit de entree kom je direct de open woonkamer binnen die naar het terras leidt. Dankzij de glazen wand is er een fantastisch uitzicht over South Beach in Florida. De keuken heeft geen deur, maar is toch een aparte ruimte. Hij is klein en praktisch en doet tevens dienst als bar.

Desde la entrada se accede directamente al salón abierto y, a través de este, a la terraza. La fachada de cristal brinda una espectacular vista de South Beach, Florida. La cocina queda separada a pesar de carecer de puerta: es muy pequeña y práctica, y también sirve de bar.

Dall'ingresso si accede direttamente al soggiorno aperto, che comunica con la terrazza. La facciata di cristallo offre una vista spettacolare su South Beach, in Florida. Pur essendo priva di porta, la cucina costituisce un ambiente separato: è molto piccola e pratica, e funge anche da bar.

A entrada dá directamente para a sala de estar em *open space*, que, por sua vez, abre para a varanda. A fachada em vidro valoriza a vista deslumbrante que se estende sobre South Beach, na Florida. A cozinha surge separada ainda que não ostente qualquer porta: pequena e prática, funciona também como bar.

Ingången öppnar upp direkt till det öppna vardagsrummet som leder till terrassen. Glasfasaden erbjuder en spektakulär utsikt över South Beach, Florida. Köket är avskilt trots att det inte har någon dörr: det är litet och praktiskt samt fungerar som en bar.

302 > 311

All Lines
MILAN, ITALY

MARCO SAVORELLI

© Matteo Piazza

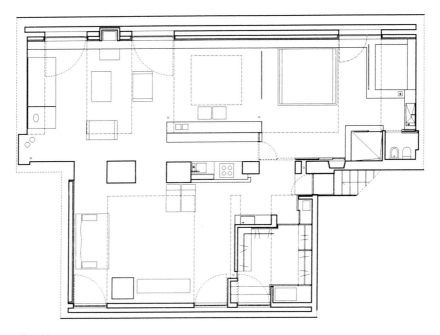

Floor plan

This attic in Milan was renovated and transformed into a modern, sophisticated, elegant loft. The furnishings chosen reflect the simple shapes, lines and minimalist style of the structural architecture.

Cet attique milanais a été rénové et transformé en un loft moderne, raffiné et élégant. Le mobilier choisi pour la décoration est en harmonie avec les lignes simples, droites et minimalistes des lieux.

Aus dieser in Mailand gelegenen Wohnung sollte durch die Renovierung ein modernes und elegantes Loft werden. Das Design des Mobiliars zeichnet sich ebenso wie die architektonische Struktur durch einfache, lineare und minimalistische Formen aus.

Deze zolderverdieping in Milaan werd gerenoveerd om er een moderne, elegante loft van te maken. Het meubilair van de inrichting is afgestemd op de eenvoudige, rechte en minimalistische vormen van de architectuur.

Este ático situado en Milán se remodeló para transformarlo en un moderno, sofisticado y elegante *loft*. El mobiliario elegido para la decoración es acorde con las formas sencillas, lineales y minimalistas de la estructura arquitectónica.

Questo attico milanese è stato ristrutturato e trasformato in un moderno loft elegante e sofisticato. Gli arredi scelti si accordano alle forme semplici, lineari e minimaliste dell'impianto architettonico.

Este sótão milanês foi renovado e transformado num *loft* moderno, elegante e sofisticado. O seu mobiliário xreflecte as formas depuradas, as linhas e o estilo minimalista patente na estrutura arquitectónica.

Det här loftet i Milano renoverades och förvandlades till ett modernt, sofistikerat, elegant loft. De valda möblerna reflekterar de enkla formerna, linjerna och den minimalistiska stilen i arkitekturen.

Ground Floor
BARCELONA, SPAIN

GCA ARCHITECTS

© José Luis Hausmann

This apartment measures approximately 70 m² and is located on the first floor of a two-storey building. The rooms are separated by sliding doors which can be opened to make the spaces larger.

Cet appartement d'environ 70 m² se trouve au rez-de-chaussée d'une maison d'un étage. Les pièces sont séparées par des portes coulissantes qui permettent d'agrandir les espaces.

Diese etwa 70 m² große Wohnung befindet sich im unteren Teil eines zweistöckigen Gebäudes. Die Zimmer werden mittels Schiebetüren voneinander abgetrennt und können so beliebig vergrößert oder verkleinert werden.

Dit appartement van ongeveer 70 m² bevindt zich op de begane grond van een gebouw van twee verdiepingen. De kamers zijn van elkaar gescheiden door schuifdeuren, waardoor ruimten naar wens groter gemaakt kunnen worden.

Este apartamento de aproximadamente 70 m² se encuentra en la parte baja de un edificio de dos plantas. Las habitaciones están separadas por puertas correderas, lo cual permite la ampliación de los ambientes.

Questo appartamento di circa 70 m² è situato nella parte bassa di un edificio di due piani. Gli ambienti sono separati da porte scorrevoli che, all'occorrenza, possono essere aperte per ampliare lo spazio.

Este apartamento tem uma área aproximada de 70 m² e está localizado no primeiro piso de um edifício de dois andares. As divisões estão separadas por portas corrediças que, abertas, aumentam a sensação de espaço.

Den här lägenheten är ungefär 70 m² och ligger på första våningen i en tvåvåningsbyggnad. Rummen avdelas med hjälp av skjutdörrar som kan öppnas upp för att göra utrymmena större.

No-Ho Loft
NEW YORK, USA

SLADE ARCHITECTS

© Jordi Miralles

Floor plan

This apartment was designed for a photographer who needed space to file and store some of his work. With all the windows in just one wall, the arrangement of the property is such that there are rooms which prevent the light reaching other areas.

Cet appartement a été conçu pour un photographe qui avait besoin d'espace pour archiver et ranger ses photos. Les fenêtres se concentrent sur un seul mur. La lumière directe n'atteint donc pas toutes les pièces.

Diese Wohnung wurde für einen Fotografen entworfen, der Wert darauf legte, genügend Platz für die Archivierung seiner Arbeiten zur Verfügung zu haben. Da sich alle Fenster an einer einzigen Wand befinden, wurde die Aufteilung der Wohnung so gestaltet, dass der Lichteinfall durch verschiedene Elemente gesteuert wird.

Dit appartement werd ontworpen voor een fotograaf die ruimte nodig had om een deel van zijn werk te archiveren en te bewaren. Er bevinden zich in slechts één muur ramen, waardoor het appartement zo kon worden ingedeeld dat sommige ruimten de lichtinval naar andere belemmeren.

Este apartamento fue diseñado para un fotógrafo con necesidad de espacio para archivar y guardar el material profesional. Como todas las ventanas se concentran en una única pared, la organización espacial está pensada para que la luz no llegue hasta algunos espacios.

Questo appartamento è stato progettato per un fotografo che aveva bisogno di spazio per archiviare e conservare una parte dei suoi lavori. Con tutte le finestre allineate lungo una parete, la disposizione degli ambienti è tale che alcune stanze impediscono ad altre di ricevere la luce.

Este apartamento foi desenhado para um fotógrafo à procura de espaço para catalogar e arquivar os seus trabalhos. Com todas as janelas na mesma parede, a disposição espacial faz com que haja divisões a impedir a passagem de luz para outras divisões.

Den här lägenheten designades till en fotograf som behövde utrymme för att arkivera och förvara några av sina verk. Med alla fönstren samlade på bara en vägg, har lägenheten ordnats på ett sådant sätt att det finns rum som hindrar ljuset från att nå andra utrymmen.

Loft Jij en Ik
BARCELONA, SPAIN

AD CASADESÚS

© AD Casadesús

Prohibido estacionar. Grac

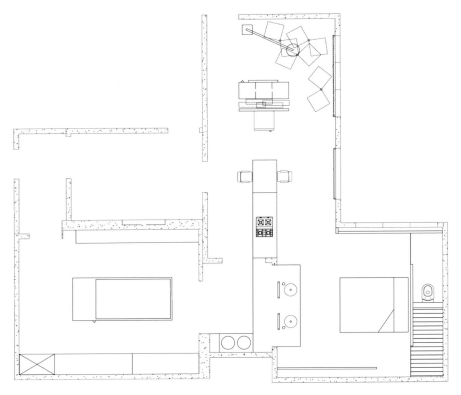

Floor plan

This apartment was designed for a young couple who often work from home and who like the sophisticated touches of modern design elements. Although the spaces are marked off, all the rooms can be reached from different angles which generates continual communication.

Cet appartement a été conçu pour un jeune couple qui y habite et y travaille, et qui aime les touches sophistiquées comme les détails de design moderne. L'espace est restreint, mais l'on accède à chaque pièce depuis un angle différent, ce qui crée une communication continue.

Diese Wohnung wurde für ein junges, zu Hause arbeitendes Paar designt. Ein eleganter Touch und einzelne, in modernem Design gehaltene Details sorgen für eine besondere Note. Trotz des begrenzten Raums kann jedes Zimmer von verschiedenen Seiten aus betreten werden – somit entsteht eine fließende, einheitliche Atmosphäre.

Dit appartement werd ontworpen voor een jong stel dat gewoonlijk thuis werkt en van geavanceerde technische snufjes en modern design houdt. De ruimten hebben beperkte afmetingen, maar doordat alle kamers van verschillende kanten toegankelijk zijn, zijn ze allemaal met elkaar verbonden.

Este apartamento se diseñó para una joven pareja que suele trabajar en la vivienda y que gusta de los toques sofisticados y de los detalles de diseño moderno. Aunque con espacios delimitados, se accede a todas las habitaciones desde diferentes ángulos, generando una continua comunicación.

Questo appartamento è stato concepito sia come abitazione che come luogo di lavoro per una giovane coppia che apprezza i dettagli sofisticati del design moderno. Nonostante lo spazio sia limitato, si può accedere a ogni stanza da angoli diversi, dando così origine a una comunicazione continua.

Este apartamento foi desenhado para um jovem casal que trabalha em casa e que aprecia a sofisticação proporcionada pelos mais modernos elementos do design. Ainda que os espaços surjam bem definidos, acedemos a todas as divisões a partir de vários ângulos, numa comunicação espacial continuada.

Den här lägenheten designades till ett ungt par som ofta arbetar hemifrån och som gillar den sofistikerade touchen som finns i moderna designelement. Trots att utrymmena är skilda från varandra, kan alla rum nås från olika vinklar, vilket gör att en ständig kommunikation skapas mellan dem.

338 ^{> 347}

338 ^{> 347}

Flatiron Loft
NEW YORK, USA

SLADE ARCHITECTS

© Jordi Miralles

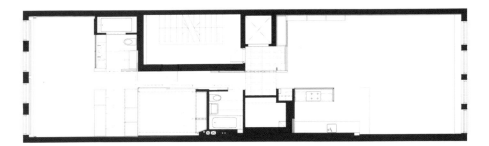

Floor plan

This rectangular loft was divided into two spaces — a private area at one end and a public one at the other, with the kitchen and the bathroom in the middle. The owners' instructions were that that accessories and furnishings should be integrated into the decoration.

Ce loft rectangulaire a été divisé en deux espaces, l'un privé et l'autre public, situés à chaque extrémité. La cuisine et la salle de bains sont disposés au centre. Les propriétaires ont souhaité que les objets et les meubles soient intégrés à la décoration.

Aus zwei verschiedenen Bereichen – den „privaten" Zimmern am einen Ende und den „öffentlichen" Räumen am anderen Ende – besteht dieses rechteckige Loft. In der Mitte befinden sich die Küche und das Badezimmer. Auf Wunsch der Bewohner sind die Accessoires und Möbelstücke Teil der Dekoration.

Deze rechthoekige loft werd verdeeld over twee zones. In het ene uiteinde bevindt zich de privézone, in het andere het gemeenschappelijke gebied. Keuken en badkamer bevinden zich in het midden. De opdracht van de bewoners luidde dat voorwerpen en meubels in de inrichting geïntegreerd moesten worden.

Este *loft* rectangular fue dividido en dos áreas: la privada, situada en uno de los extremos, y la pública, ubicada en el otro. La cocina y el cuarto de baño se situaron en el centro. El deseo expresado por los propietarios era que los objetos y los muebles estuvieran integrados en la decoración.

Questo loft rettangolare è stato diviso in due spazi: un'area privata da una parte e un'area pubblica dall'altra, con il bagno e la cucina al centro. Il proprietario ha stabilito che mobili e accessori dovessero essere parte integrante della decorazione.

Este *loft* rectangular foi dividido em dois espaços – uma zona privada de um dos lados e, do outro lado, uma zona social, com a cozinha e a casa de banho. Os proprietários expressaram o desejo de ver o mobiliário e os acessórios serem integrados na decoração.

Det här rektangulära loftet delades upp på två utrymmen – en avskild yta på den ena sidan, och en allmän yta på den andra, med köket och badrummet i mitten. Ägarens önskan var att tillbehör och möbler skulle integreras med dekorationen.

Bold Time
LONDON, UK

TARGET LIVING

© Philip Vile

It was important to separate the domestic areas within the limited space of this apartment, so different spaces were created in which to sleep, to eat and to relax. One of the main characteristics of the property is the elevated platform which houses the bedroom, distinguishing it from the other areas of the property.

Dans cet espace restreint, il était essentiel de séparer clairement les différentes zones. On a donc créé des espaces particuliers pour dormir, manger et se détendre. La chambre, dissimulée derrière un fin rideau, est surélevée.

In dieser recht kleinen Wohnung war es vor allem wichtig, die Nutzungsbereiche deutlich voneinander zu unterschieden; so entstanden verschiedene Zonen zum Schlafen, Essen und Entspannen. Eine Besonderheit der Wohnung bildet die erhöhte Plattform, die das Schlafzimmer von den anderen Bereichen abgrenzt.

Aangezien de verschillende functies van deze beperkte ruimte duidelijk van elkaar gescheiden moesten worden, zijn er aparte zones voor slapen, eten en ontspanning gecreëerd. Een van de opvallendste elementen is het verhoogde platform voor de slaapkamer, waardoor de andere zones van de woning goed uitkomen.

Era fundamental separar claramente las áreas domésticas de este espacio limitado, por lo que se crearon distintas zonas para dormir, comer y relajarse. Una de las principales características es una plataforma elevada para el dormitorio, que permite la distinción de las demás áreas de la vivienda.

Era importante riuscire a mantenere separate le aree private all'interno di questo piccolo appartamento, perciò sono stati creati spazi differenti in cui dormire, desinare e rilassarsi. Una delle caratteristiche principali dell'abitazione è la piattaforma sopraelevata che ospita la camera da letto e la distingue dal resto dell'appartamento.

Era importante separar as diferentes zonas habitacionais deste apartamento, pelo que foram criados espaços de repouso, de convívio e de refeições. Uma das principais características da casa reside na plataforma elevada que abriga o quarto e que o separa das restantes zonas da casa.

Koska tämän pienen huoneiston käyttötilat oli tärkeä erottaa selvästi, luotiin erilliset alueet nukkumiseen, syömiseen ja rentoutumiseen. Yksi pääpiirteistä on makuutilan korotettu taso, mikä tekee siitä erilaisen asunnon muihin osiin verrattuna.

Cool Passion
TUNG CHUNG, HONG KONG, CHINA

ANTHONY CHAN

370 > 381

Pink House
ROME, ITALY

FILIPPO BOMBACE

© Luigi Filetici

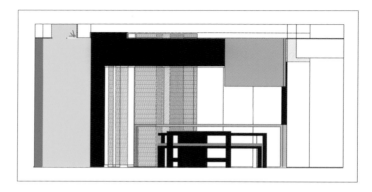

Section

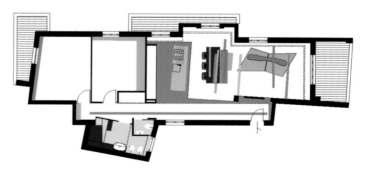

Floor plan

The color and the light in this apartment, located in Rome in a building from the 1950s, played an important part in the design. The idea was to transform the spaces, and this was achieved by using movable partitions made of translucent materials in tones of pink and purple.

La couleur et la lumière ont joué un rôle essentiel dans l'aménagement de cet appartement situé dans un immeuble romain des années 1950. L'intention était de créer un espace transformable, et l'on a eu recours à des cloisons mobiles translucides roses et pourpres.

Licht und Farben spielten bei der Konzeption dieser in einem römischen 50er-Jahre-Gebäude gelegenen Wohnung eine Schlüsselrolle. Es wurde versucht, veränderbare Räume zu schaffen – dafür griff man auf bewegliche, aus lichtdurchlässigen Materialien gefertigte Raumteiler in den Farbtönen Rosa und Purpur zurück.

Dit appartement is gelegen in Rome, in een gebouw uit de jaren vijftig. Kleur en licht speelden een beslissende rol in het ontwerp. Om de vertrekken flexibel te maken werd gekozen voor verplaatsbare afscheidingen van doorzichtig materiaal in roze- en paarstinten.

El color y la luz en este apartamento, situado en un edificio de los años cincuenta en Roma, jugaron un papel decisivo a la hora de diseñarlo. La idea era que los ambientes se pudieran transformar fácilmente, por lo que se recurrió a separadores movibles, en tonos rosas y púrpuras, de materiales traslúcidos.

Il colore e la luce hanno giocato un ruolo decisivo nel design di questo appartamento, situato a Roma in un edificio degli anni cinquanta. Allo scopo di trasformare gli ambienti ci si è avvalsi di partizioni mobili dai toni rosa e porpora in materiali traslucidi.

A cor e a luz deste apartamento, situado em Roma num edifício dos anos 50, desempenharam um papel importante na sua remodelação. Neste projecto, visou-se sobretudo a transformação dos espaços existentes, o que foi conseguido através do recurso a separadores amovíveis em tons rosa e roxo.

Färgen och ljuset i den här lägenheten, som finns i Rom i en byggnad från 50-talet, spelade en viktig roll i designen. Idén var att förvandla utrymmena, och detta uppnåddes genom att man använde sig av flyttbara skiljeväggar gjorda av halvgenomskinliga material i rosa och lila nyanser.

382 [>] 389

Calypso Hill
OOSTDUINKERKE, BELGIUM

NON KISTCH GRIUP

© Jan Verlinde

Completely surrounded by windows, this Calypso Hill apartment in Belgium is remarkable for the harmony of the colors and the post-modern architecture. A spiral staircase leads to a terrace on the upper level.

Cet appartement de Calypso Hill, en Belgique, se distingue par l'harmonie de ses couleurs et son architecture postmoderne. On accède à la terrasse de l'étage supérieur par un escalier en colimaçon.

Diese komplett von Glas umgebene Wohnung auf dem Berg Calypso in Belgien überzeugt durch eine perfekte Farbharmonie sowie durch ihre postmoderne Architektur. Im obersten Stockwerk befindet sich eine Terrasse, die über eine Wendeltreppe betreten werden kann.

De muren van dit appartement van project Calypso Hill in België zijn volledig van glas. De harmonieuze kleuren en de postmoderne architectuur zijn opvallend. Op de bovenverdieping bevindt zich een terras dat te bereiken is via een wenteltrap.

Rodeado completamente por cristalera, este apartamento de Calypso Hill, en Bélgica, destaca por la armonía en los colores y la arquitectura posmoderna. En el nivel superior se encuentra una terraza a la que se accede a través de una escalera de caracol.

Completamente circondato da vetrate, questo appartamento di Calypso Hill, in Belgio, risalta per l'armonia dei colori e per la sua architettura postmoderna. Al piano superiore si trova una terrazza alla quale si accede mediante una scala a chiocciola.

Integralmente rodeado de vidro, este apartamento no empreendimento Calyspo Hill, na Bélgica, destaca-se pela harmonia criada pelas cores e a arquitectura pós-moderna. Uma escada em espiral conduz-nos ao terraço situado no piso superior.

Den här lägenheten, som är helt och hållet omgiven av glas, ligger på Calypso Hill i Belgien, och är anmärkningsvärd för färgernas harmoni och den postmodernistiska arkitekturen. En spiraltrappa leder till en terrass på den översta våningen.

390 ^{> 399}

Apartment on Central Park
NEW YORK, USA

BONETTI/KOZERSKI STUDIO

© Matteo Piazza

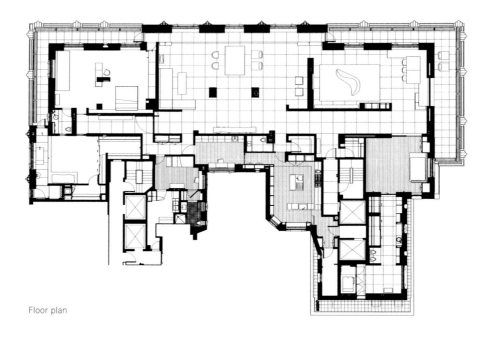

Floor plan

Comprising a kitchen, a dining room, a meditation room, a sauna, an office and a bedroom with *en suite* bathroom and dressing room, this apartment affords spectacular views of Central Park and New York City.

Cet appartement comporte une cuisine, une salle à manger, une pièce réservée à la méditation, un sauna, un bureau et une chambre avec une salle de bains et un dressing. Il donne une vue spectaculaire sur Central Park et sur New York.

Von dieser Wohnung aus, die Küche, Esszimmer, Meditationsraum, Sauna, Büro und Schlafzimmer mit En-suite-Badezimmer und begehbarem Kleiderschrank enthält, kann eine spektakuläre Aussicht auf den Central Park und die Stadt New York genossen werden.

Dit appartement bestaat uit een keuken, eetkamer, meditatiekamer, sauna, kantoor en een slaapkamer en suite met badkamer en kleedkamer. Het heeft een schitterend uitzicht op Central Park en op de stad New York.

Compuesto por una cocina, un comedor, una estancia para meditación, una sauna, una oficina y un dormitorio con baño y vestidor, este piso disfruta de la espectacular vista del Central Park y de la ciudad de Nueva York.

Costituito da una cucina, una sala da pranzo, una stanza per la meditazione, una sauna, uno studio e una camera da letto con bagno e cabina armadio, questo appartamento gode di una vista spettacolare su Central Park e New York.

Composto por uma cozinha, uma sala de jantar, uma sala de meditação, uma sauna, um escritório e um quarto com casa de banho e zona de vestir, este apartamento desfruta de uma vista estonteante sobre o Central Park e a cidade de Nova Iorque.

Den här lägenheten, som omfattar kök, matsal, meditationsrum, bastu, kontor, samt ett sovrum med inbyggt badrum och omklädningsrum, erbjuder en hänförande utsikt över Central Park och New York City.

400 > 409

Stewart Loft
NEW YORK, USA

JAMES GAUER

The strong, thick walls with bookshelves create a separation around the edge of the room. The interior doors are made of translucent glass with aluminum frames, allowing light to flow through into the bedroom but maintaining privacy.

Les étagères épaisses et résistantes où sont rangés les livres font office de cloison de séparation entre les pièces. Pour laisser entrer la lumière dans la chambre tout en préservant l'intimité, les portes intérieures sont en verre translucide, avec des cadres en aluminium.

Die robusten und dicken Wände dienen als Raumteiler und zugleich als Aufbewahrungsort für Bücher. Um den Lichteinfall auch im Schlafzimmer zu ermöglichen und gleichzeitig die Privatsphäre zu wahren, wurden Milchglastüren mit Aluminiumrahmen verwendet.

De solide, dikke wanden waarin boeken zijn opgeborgen, doen dienst als de muren van de kamers. Voor lichtinval in de slaapkamer zijn lichtdoorlatende glazen binnendeuren met een aluminium frame gebruikt die voldoende privacy bieden.

Las resistentes y gruesas paredes que sirven como almacenamiento de libros hacen de separador del perímetro de las habitaciones. Para permitir el paso de la luz hacia el dormitorio, y a la vez preservar la intimidad, las puertas interiores son de vidrio translúcido con marcos de aluminio.

Le pareti spesse e resistenti con gli scaffali per i libri hanno la funzione di delimitare il perimetro del locale. Per consentire il passaggio della luce nella camera da letto pur mantenendo l'intimità, le porte interne sono realizzate in vetro traslucido con telai in alluminio.

As paredes fortes e espessas com estantes criam uma separação junto ao canto da divisão. De forma a permitir que a luz fluísse livremente pelo quarto, mantendo simultaneamente a privacidade, as portas interiores são de vidro translúcido com caixilhos em alumínio.

De starka, tjocka väggarna med bokhyllor fungerar som avdelare vid rummets ytterkanter. För att släppa in ljus till sovrummet och samtidigt behålla avskildheten, har man valt dörrar av halvgenomskinligt glas med aluminiumramar.

410 ^{> 421}

Loft in Ciutat Vella
BARCELONA, SPAIN

MARÍA VIVES, LLUÍS ESCARMIS/GCA ARQUITECTES

© Jordi Miralles

Night and Day
ANTWERP, BELGIUM

VINCENT VAN DUYSEN ARCHITECTS

© Jan Verlinde

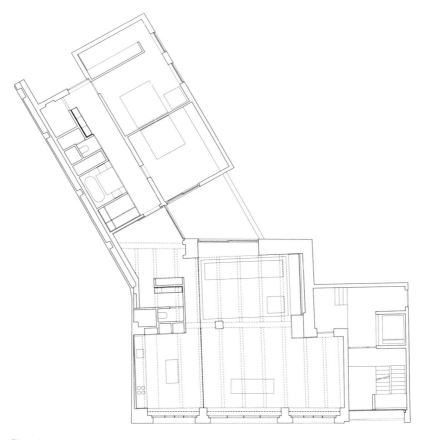

Floor plan

The design for this apartment was drawn up with the uses of the two spaces in mind. The space was divided in half to create a daytime area near the windows and a night-time area in the interior of the property.

Ce logement a été conçu en tenant compte de la fonction des pièces. Il a été divisé en deux zones : l'une pour le jour, située face aux baies vitrées, et l'autre pour la nuit, plus à l'intérieur de l'appartement.

Während der Konzeption dieser Wohnung wurde vor allem der praktische Aspekt berücksichtigt. Sie ist in zwei Bereiche eingeteilt: Der eine an der Fensterfront gelegene Bereich wird am Tage genutzt, der andere im Inneren der Wohnung dient der Nutzung bei Nacht.

Bij het ontwerp van dit appartement werd uitgegaan van de functies van de verschillende ruimten. De woning werd over twee zones verdeeld: die voor overdag grenst aan de grote ramen en die voor 's nachts ligt binnen in het appartement.

El diseño de este piso se concibió teniendo en cuenta la funcionalidad de los ambientes. Se dividió en dos áreas: una para el día, situada frente a los ventanales, y otra para la noche, en la parte más interior del apartamento.

Per il design di questo appartamento si è tenuto conto della funzionalità degli ambienti. Lo spazio è stato diviso in due: una zona giorno, di fronte alle vetrate, e una zona notte, all'interno.

Este apartamento foi concebido tendo-se em consideração a funcionalidade dos dois ambientes. O espaço foi dividido a meio para criar uma área diurna junto às janelas e uma área nocturna no interior da casa.

Designen i den här lägenheten utarbetades med de två utrymmenas funktionalitet i åtanke. Utrymmet delades på hälften för att skapa en yta nära fönstren, som kunde användas under dagtid, och en yta för nattetid i lägenhetens inre del.

Loft in Milan
MILAN, ITALY

LAURA AGNOLETTO & MARZIO RUSCONI CLIRICI

© Matteo Piazza

The areas most commonly used during the day in this apartment have been carefully outlined with furniture, as there is a circular route around the property through open spaces. In the middle are the bathroom and the kitchen, and the bedrooms are on the upper floor.

Les pièces les plus utilisées en journée sont délimitées par le mobilier, car dans cet appartement la circulation se fait en cercle, à travers des pièces ouvertes. La salle de bains et la cuisine se trouvent au milieu, et les chambres sont à l'étage supérieur.

Eine Art Rundweg verbindet die offenen Räume dieser Wohnung miteinander. Die am Tag häufig genutzten Zimmer werden durch das Mobiliar voneinander abgegrenzt. In der Mitte liegen das Bad und die Küche, während im obersten Stockwerk die Schlafzimmer angesiedelt sind.

De kamers van dit appartement die overdag het meest gebruikt worden, worden vooral begrensd door meubilair. Doordat de ruimten open zijn gehouden, is er sprake van een doorlopende route in de woning. In het midden bevinden zich badkamer en keuken, op de bovenverdieping de slaapkamers.

Los ambientes de este apartamento más utilizados durante el día se encuentran especialmente delimitados por el mobiliario, ya que el piso posee un recorrido circular a través de espacios abiertos. En el centro se encuentran el cuarto de baño y la cocina, y en el piso superior, los dormitorios.

I locali più utilizzati durante il giorno sono delimitati principalmente dai mobili, quasi a creare un percorso circolare attraverso gli ambienti aperti. Il bagno e la cucina sono situati al centro, mentre le camere da letto si trovano al piano superiore.

As áreas deste loft mais utilizadas durante o dia foram cuidadosamente delimitadas com mobiliário, na medida em que o apartamento permite que se siga um percurso circular através dos seus espaços abertos. No seu centro estão localizadas a casa de banho e a cozinha, enquanto os quartos se encontram no piso superior.

I den här lägenheten är det möjligt att gå runt genom öppna utrymmen. Därför har de under dagtid mest använda utrymmena avgränsats noggrant med hjälp av möbler. I mitten finns badrum och kök, och sovrummen återfinns på övervåningen.

Los Cerros Apartment
BOGOTÁ, COLOMBIA

GUILLERMO ARIAS

© Eduardo Consuegra, Pablo Rojas, Álvaro Gutiérrez

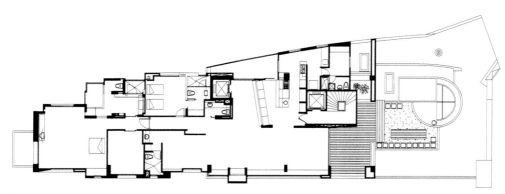

Floor plan

Located in a mountainous region on the outskirts of Bogota, this apartment looks out on two different views. The bedrooms and bathrooms face east, overlooking the forest and the mountains, while the view from the living room is to the west towards the city.

Situé dans les faubourgs de Bogotá, dans une zone montagneuse, cet appartement offre à ses habitants deux vues différentes. Les chambres et les salles de bains donnent à l'est, sur la jungle et les collines environnantes, tandis que le salon est orienté vers la ville à l'ouest.

Im Umland Bogotás in einer Berglandschaft gelegen, bietet diese Wohnung zwei verschiedene Aussichten. Von den nach Osten hin liegenden Schlaf- und Badezimmern aus sieht man den Wald und die Berge, während sich vom Wohnzimmer aus nach Westen hin der Blick auf die Stadt öffnet.

Dit appartement bevindt zich in een bergachtige omgeving buiten Bogotá en biedt de bewoners aan twee kanten uitzicht. Slaapkamers en badkamers zien uit op het oosten, waar het woud en de omringende bergen te zien zijn. Het uitzicht vanuit de woonkamer aan de westkant laat de stad zien.

Situado en los alrededores de la ciudad de Bogotá y en una zona montañosa, este piso brinda a sus habitantes dos vistas diferentes. Los dormitorios y baños dan hacia el este, y desde allí se aprecian la selva y las sierras de alrededor. La vista del oeste, desde la sala de estar, permite contemplar la ciudad.

Situato in una zona montuosa alla periferia di Bogotà, questo appartamento offre due diversi viste panoramiche. Le camere da letto e i bagni sono sul lato est, da cui si gode il paesaggio della foresta e delle catene montuose circostanti. Il soggiorno, a ovest, si affaccia invece sulla città.

Situado numa região montanhosa na periferia de Bogotá, este apartamento desfruta de duas vistas diferentes. Enquanto os quartos e as casas de banho estão voltados para leste, contemplando a floresta e as montanhas envolventes, a partir da sala de estar é possível apreciar a cidade, a oeste.

I en bergig region i utkanten av Bogotá, finns den här lägenheten som vetter mot två olika håll. Sovrummen och badrummen vetter mot öst, med utsikt över skogen och bergen, medan vardagsrummet erbjuder västlig utsikt mot staden.

452 > 459

Apartment in Milan
MILAN, ITALY

LUCA ROLLA

© Andrea Martiradonna

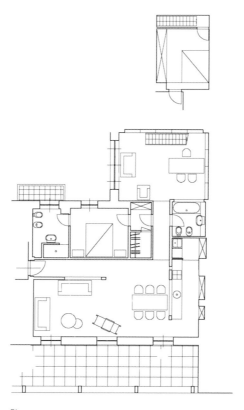

Plans

Located in an old office block which has been converted into a residential complex, this apartment has spaces for living and for working. Using walls with openings, the renovation created marked day and night-time areas, while at the same time maintaining a certain continuity between the spaces.

Situé dans un ancien immeuble de bureaux converti en complexe résidentiel, cet appartement est composé d'espaces pour vivre et pour travailler. Grâce à des blocs de murs percés d'ouvertures, la rénovation a défini des espaces pour la nuit et pour la journée tout en conservant une certaine continuité entre les pièces.

In einem ehemaligen, in einen Wohnkomplex umgewandelten Bürogebäude in Mailand wurde hier eine Kombination aus Wohn- und Arbeitsraum geschaffen. Dank der vorhandenen, mit Öffnungen versehenen Wände konnten die Tages- und Nachtbereiche voneinander abgegrenzt werden, ohne die Einheit des Raumes zu zerstören.

Dit appartement met woon- en werkruimten bevindt zich in een voormalig kantoorgebouw dat is omgebouwd tot appartementencomplex. Er zijn wandblokken met openingen gebruikt om de ruimten voor overdag en 's nachts van elkaar te scheiden. Niettemin is een zekere continuïteit tussen de ruimten behouden.

Situado en un antiguo edificio de oficinas, ahora convertido en un complejo residencial, el piso posee espacios para vivir y trabajar. A través de bloques de paredes con huecos, la renovación estableció espacios delimitados para la noche y el día, aunque manteniendo cierta continuidad entre los ambientes.

Situato in un antico palazzo di uffici trasformato in complesso residenziale, l'appartamento è composto da spazi abitativi e lavorativi. Tramite delle aperture sulle pareti divisorie, la ristrutturazione ha creato una zona notte separata da quella giorno, pur mantenendo una certa continuità fra le due aree.

Situado num velho edifício de escritórios que foi reconvertido num complexo residencial, este apartamento conta com áreas de trabalho e de habitação. Com aberturas nas paredes, a renovação criou uma marcada distinção entre áreas diurnas e nocturnas, mantendo, ainda assim, uma certa continuidade entre os espaços.

I en gammal kontorsbyggnad som har förvandlats till ett bostadskomplex ligger den här lägenheten, som har anpassats för att bli bostad och arbetsplats. Genom att använda sig av väggar med öppningar, markeras ytor som används dag- respektive nattetid, och samtidigt upprätthålls en viss helhet i hela utrymmet.

460 > 469

Fraternitat Duplex
BARCELONA, SPAIN

JOAN BACH

© Jordi Miralles

This property in Barcelona has a mezzanine which houses the living room. The interior design was based on simplicity and the prominence of color. Red, white and black combine in the furnishings, with grey, beige and white on the structural elements of the apartment.

Cette résidence barcelonaise est dotée d'une mezzanine que les occupants utilisent comme pièce à vivre. La décoration est basée sur des principes de simplicité et de prédominance de la couleur. Le rouge, le blanc et le noir se combinent sur les meubles, et le gris, le beige et le blanc sur la structure de l'appartement.

Die Besonderheit dieser in Barcelona gelegenen Wohnung bildet ein Mezzanin, das als Wohnzimmer genutzt wird. Das Innendesign wurde nach den Kriterien Schlichtheit und Dominanz der Farben gestaltet. Rot, Weiß und Schwarz bilden die Farben der Möbel und Grau, Beige und Weiß die der restlichen Wohnungsausstattung.

Deze woning in Barcelona beschikt over een mezzanine die als woonkamer wordt gebruikt. Bij het interieurontwerp vormden eenvoud en kleur de uitgangspunten. De kleuren rood, wit en zwart zijn gecombineerd in de meubels, terwijl grijs, beige en wit te vinden zijn in de afwerking van het appartement zelf.

Esta residencia, situada en Barcelona, posee un altillo que se utiliza como sala de estar. El diseño interior se realizó considerando la premisa de simplicidad y la prominencia del color. Rojo, blanco y negro combinan en los muebles, y gris, *beige* y blanco en la estructura del piso.

In questa abitazione situata a Barcellona è stato realizzato un ammezzato che ospita il soggiorno. Per il design degli interni si è scelto di basarsi sulla semplicità e sulla preponderanza del colore. Nei mobili troviamo una combinazione di rosso, bianco e nero, mentre gli elementi strutturali dell'appartamento si caratterizzano per i toni del grigio, del beige e del bianco.

Este apartamento em Barcelona dispõe de uma *mezzanine* onde se situa a sala de estar. Na concepção dos interiores, teve-se o cuidado de destacar a simplicidade e a proeminência da cor. Os tons vermelhos, brancos e pretos do mobiliário combinam com o castanho, o bege e o branco dos elementos estruturais do apartamento.

I den här bostaden som finns i Barcelona, finns en mezzanin som rymmer vardagsrummet. Inredningsdesignen grundar sig på enkelhet och de utmärkande färgerna. Rött, vitt och svart i möblerna kombineras med grått, beige och vitt i byggnadselementen i lägenheten.

Blossoming Interior
HONG KONG, CHINA

IPPOLITO FLEITZ GROUP

© Zooey Braun

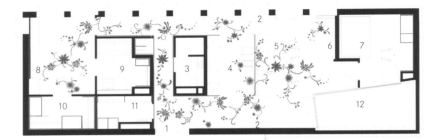

Floor plan

1. Entry
2. Hallway
3. Bathroom
4. Kitchen
5. Dining room/office
6. Living room
7. Guest room
8. Master bedroom
9. Master bathroom
10. Dressing room
11. Mirrored closet
12. Balcony

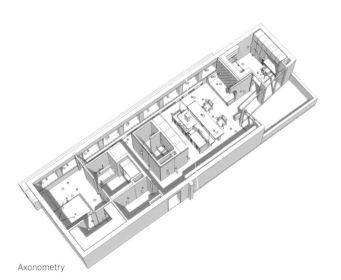

Axonometry

The shape of the apartment is an elongated rectangle with a long entrance hall at each end. A feeling of calm and organization has been created by the use of cubic shapes with defined lines, the uniformity of the materials for the furniture, and the oak floor.

Cet appartement est un rectangle allongé avec deux entrées situées à chaque extrémité. On a voulu donner une impression de calme et d'organisation avec les formes cubiques aux lignes nettes et l'uniformité des matériaux des meubles et du sol en chêne.

Ein längliches Rechteck mit zwei großen Eingangsbereichen an je einem Ende der Wohnung bildet die Grundform dieser Wohnung. Kubische Formen und dezente Linien sowie die Einheitlichkeit der Möbel und Eichenböden vermitteln einen Eindruck von Ruhe und Klarheit.

Deze woning heeft de vorm van een lange rechthoek met twee grote entreeruimten aan beide uiteinden. Dankzij de strakke lijnen van de blokvormen, het meubilair van één soort materiaal en de eiken vloeren is er een sfeer van overzicht en rust ontstaan.

La disposición consiste básicamente en un rectángulo alargado con dos recibidores que se ubican a cada uno de los lados del piso. Con el uso de formas cúbicas de líneas definidas y la uniformidad del material en los muebles y suelos, ambos en roble, se buscó la sensación de orden y tranquilidad.

Fondamentalmente, l'appartamento ha la forma di un rettangolo allungato con un ampio ingresso situato su ciascuna delle due estremità. L'utilizzo di forme cubiche dalle linee definite, l'uniformità dei materiali con cui sono realizzati i mobili e i pavimenti in rovere trasmettono una sensazione di calma e organizzazione.

Este apartamento tem a forma de um rectângulo alongado, com um espaçoso hall de entrada em cada uma das pontas. O ambiente calmo e organizado do espaço resulta das suas formas cúbicas e linhas definidas, da uniformidade dos materiais do mobiliário e do pavimento em carvalho.

Lägenheten har formats likt en vidsträckt rektangel med en lång ingångshall på vardera ände. En känsla av lugn och ordning har skapats genom användandet av kubiska former med definierade linjer, enligheten i möblernas material, samt ekgolvet.

Duplex in Born
BARCELONA, SPAIN

JOAN PONS FORMENT

This luxurious, sophisticated apartment in the Born neighborhood of Barcelona is remarkable for the extreme contrast between black and white, and the combination of the two. The staircase not only gives access to the bedroom and the home office on the upper floor, but is also a decorative element.

Cet appartement luxueux et élégant du quartier du Born à Barcelone se distingue par le contraste intense entre le blanc et le noir, et la combinaison de ces deux couleurs. L'escalier qui donne accès à la chambre et au bureau de l'étage supérieur est en lui-même un élément de décoration.

Diese luxuriös-elegante Wohnung in der Stadt Born nahe Barcelona zeichnet sich einerseits durch die auffälligen Kontraste, anderseits durch die Kombination von Schwarz und Weiß aus. Neben ihrer Funktion als Zugang zum Schlafzimmer und zum Heimbüro im oberen Stockwerk dient die Treppe vor allem als Dekorationselement.

Dit luxueuze, smaakvolle appartement in de wijk Born in Barcelona valt op door het grote contrast tussen zwart en wit en de combinatie van deze kleuren. De trap geeft niet alleen toegang tot de slaapkamer en het kantoor aan huis op de bovenverdieping, maar is ook een decoratief element op zich.

Este lujoso y sofisticado apartamento del barrio barcelonés del Born destaca por el marcado contraste entre el blanco y el negro, y la combinación de ambos. La escalera, además de dar acceso al dormitorio y al *home-office* de la planta alta, constituye en sí misma un elemento de decoración.

Questo appartamento lussuoso e raffinato del barrio barcellonese del Born si distingue per il forte contrasto fra il bianco e il nero e per la combinazione dei due colori. La scala, oltre a permettere l'accesso alla camera da letto e allo studio del piano superiore, costituisce di per sé un elemento decorativo.

Este luxuoso e sofisticado apartamento do bairro de Born, em Barcelona, destaca-se pelo contraste extremo estabelecido pelo preto e pelo branco, bem como pela combinação de ambos. A escada permite aceder ao quarto e ao escritório, no piso superior, mas é também um elemento decorativo.

Den här lyxiga, sofistikerade lägenheten i bostadskvarteret Born i Barcelona är anmärkningsvärd på grund av den extrema kontrasten mellan svart och vitt, samt på grund av kombinationen mellan dem båda. Trappan ger tillträde till sovrummet och bostadskontoret på övervåningen, samt är även ett dekorativt inslag.

Silverman Residentie

SCOTTDALE, ARIZONA, USA

MICHAEL P. JOHNSON DESIGN STUDIOS

© Bill Timmermann

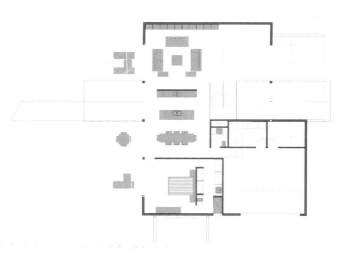

Lower floor plan

Upper floor plan